DEEPEN
your
FRIENDSHIP
with
GOD

A 52-WEEK
DEVOTIONAL
JOURNEY

Faith Eury Cho

Ink &
Willow

Published in the United States by Ink & Willow, an imprint of Random House, a division of Penguin Random House LLC.

INK & WILLOW and colophon are registered trademarks of Penguin Random House LLC.

Interior illustrations: shutterstock.com: optimarc, spiral brushstroke texture; AlexZaitsev, curved brushstrokes; Rufiyana Nikitushkina, abstract strokes; KarolinaCreate, squiggle line art; dimpank, grainy ink splatter; AnastasiyaS, brushstroke art; MURRIRA, abstract organic shapes; Irina Davydenko, abstract flower shapes

Hardback ISBN 978-0-593-79740-2

Printed in Malaysia

inkandwillow.com

9 8 7 6 5 4 3 2 1

First Edition

Book and cover design by Danielle Deschenes

Cover art: shutterstock.com: Zikatuha, cyanotype petals; Sneguole, cyanotype leaves; MURRIRA, organic shapes

Most Ink & Willow books are available at special quantity discounts for bulk purchase for premiums, fundraising, and corporate and educational needs by organizations, churches, and businesses. Special books or book excerpts also can be created to fit specific needs. For details, contact specialmarketscms@penguinrandomhouse.com.

To my extraordinary husband,
Dave, with whom I've laughed
through both mountaintops
and valleys.

CONTENTS

INTRODUCTION

You reveal the path of life to me;
in your presence is abundant joy;
at your right hand are eternal pleasures.

PSALM 16:11

Joy is one of the most universally sought-after experiences of our existence. Some people spend their entire lives in pursuit of it, pay a high price to feel it, and often settle for imitations of it. The word *joy*—or the renditions of *joy* such as *joyous, joyful,* or *rejoice*—is mentioned more than four hundred times in the Bible. The majority of these mentions relate to experiencing friendship with God.[1] Whether joy comes through adoring who He is or celebrating the work of His hands, the Bible makes clear that we were never meant to be fulfilled on earth without our creator. If you long to have this kind of joy in life, then enjoying friendship with God is worthy of exploration. This fifty-two-week devotional journey is a start toward that intention.

Because to know Jesus is to enjoy Him.

This is possible because a transcendent and omnipresent God chooses to be immanent and accessible. This is what I refer to as "the Presence of God." God is everywhere, but He made a way to be spiritually and relationally present with you. God Himself is unconditionally present, thanks to the sacrifice of Christ. We can interact with the Holy Spirit like a friend, and He loyally remains with us no matter the circumstance. Although He is infinite, He is knowable, and our knowledge of Him can grow forever. Our enjoyment of Him can grow forever as well.

Now, friend of God, by the word *enjoy*, I do not mean a transient kind of gratification, like the indulgent pleasures we often pine for. Although abandoning yourself to gluttony, luxurious spending, and carnal cravings may offer moments of what can feel like happiness, I speak of a more reliable force. By *enjoy*, I also do not speak of adrenaline or hype, such as what you might feel when achieving your life goals or getting swept up in romantic chemistry. Instead, I mean the supernatural kind of enjoyment—a deep and vitalizing fulfillment. It is the kind that your body craves and your soul draws life from. To enjoy the Presence of God does not mean that your days will be immune to burdensome sighs and sorrowful tears. Until heaven, we will always be missing something while on earth. But even so, enjoying friendship with God keeps your fire of faith ablaze, regardless of the storm that howls around you. It keeps you standing upright in a fallen world and loving brightly in the thick of darkness.

Before we begin, I would love to offer guidance on how to use this journal. The goal of each week's devotional is to guide you directly to Scripture and in communing with the Holy Spirit yourself. We will explore biblical revelation through three sections: Enjoying Salvation, Enjoying His Presence, and Enjoying His Friendship in Prisons, Storms, and Everything Mundane. The first purpose of these sections is to fortify the foundation of our friendship with the Holy Spirit by enriching our understanding of our salvation in Christ. From there, we will explore the endless wealth of His Presence, deepening our satisfaction in Him. Last, we will continue to exercise our spiritual awareness of His goodness no matter the season we are in today.

Don't be pressured to perform. If anything, I encourage you to do these devotionals wherever you feel most at ease. Whether in the quiet of your room with scented candles or in the hustle and bustle of a café, the Holy Spirit is wherever you are. There is room to write on the pages, but do not allow the lines to limit you. Just let the questions and the space spur you on to open yourself to Him. The only requirement is to show up with your honesty as you approach the words that follow. Scribble, doodle, or wash the pages with tears if you must.

Each devotional will guide you to the following interactions with Jesus.

THE THOUGHT OF THE DAY

As we approach Him, it is not always easy to turn off the noise around us and within us. The Thought of the Day helps us take hold of our minds for Jesus. It is a means to turn down life's volume so that you can allow your soul to be present with Him. It also primes you for the Scripture of the week. Consider this a warm-up for your soul.

ACKNOWLEDGE JESUS

Before you engage with anyone on a personal level, it makes sense to first greet them or acknowledge their presence. Take a deep breath here and clear your mind. Sometimes, that's the hardest part—clearing our minds. It may feel uncomfortable at first if you are used to constantly worrying, planning, or keeping an eye on your phone for notifications. But here, you can shift your attention to Him. Consider every good gift He's given in your life. Spend time thanking Him. After you consider what He's done, ponder who He is. Allow your soul to gaze at His goodness and spend time in adoration. This is a personal letter to your friend Jesus, so you do not need to sound extra spiritual or poetic. Feel free to speak plainly to Him through these pages. Allow your mind to be engulfed by who He is and His nearness to you.

POUR OUT YOUR HEART

What was at the forefront of your heart as you greeted Jesus? Take a moment of silence and stillness here. Notice what bubbles up from within you. What are you carrying? What concerns you? What are you tied down with? What pokes and prods at you? Pour this out to God. Be as candid as possible, and take your time. If you feel yourself struggling here, you can even say this portion out loud. Don't worry about having this part make sense. You're not writing an essay. This is not a test. You are just expressing your heart to your Father, and you are safe.

MEDITATE ON SCRIPTURE

Each week will be assigned a passage of Scripture, so always try to keep your Bible handy! As you read the passage of the week, what parts stick out to you? Writing down the words and verses that draw your attention can awaken your soul because you are acting on what you are reading. Allow the Holy Spirit to speak to you here. Don't try to investigate the context and meaning quite yet. We'll do that soon after. In my book *Experiencing Friendship with God,* I mention, "Meditating on the Bible allows you to acknowledge God, consider Him, and make room for Him to minister to your heart. You may not always feel it, but it is nourishing your soul. It is a violent disruption and eradication of toxic ways of thinking."[2] Just allow the truth to sit in your mind and seep into your heart. Dwell and marinate here. Be ready to highlight, copy verses to your phone, and save what really spoke to you. You can even meditate on the passage of the week after your devotional is over. Take a picture of it. Keep your Bible open to it as a reminder.

REFLECT

This is the part where we step into a brief investigation and study. An accurate understanding of God's Word helps us better hear Him and understand His will. May this portion deepen your knowledge of God's heart and character. Psalm 1:1–2 says,

> How happy is the one who does not
> walk in the advice of the wicked
> or stand in the pathway with sinners
> or sit in the company of mockers!
> Instead, his delight is in the LORD's instruction,
> and he meditates on it day and night.

Joy and life are produced when you hold fast to His truth, which is why it is worth our while to understand it in depth. If you feel led to, you can even take a pause after reading this portion to allow the Holy Spirit to speak to you again. How does the Scripture for the week reveal your heart? How does it offer wisdom to your current situation? What are your takeaways and applications from it?

PRAY

Respond to God here. Don't be too caught up with proprieties; instead, use your own words to respond to Him in your most authentic way. In addition, this is also the space to make your petitions. Ask for help where you need it. Bring up your needs and concerns. You can petition on behalf of others as well. What's wonderful about this part is that you can always look back later to reflect on how God answered your prayers. This further enriches our enjoyment of His friendship!

Now, let us begin.

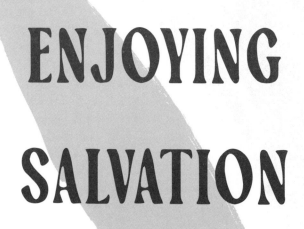

ENJOYING

SALVATION

WEEK  1

WHERE ARE YOU?

Where is your heart today, friend? I know we are not having a real conversation here because I am the author and you are my beloved reader. But bear with me because this is very important.

Where is your heart?

What goes on in your heart matters because our journey to enjoying friendship with God starts there. It matters because the condition of your heart speaks volumes to where you are in relation to Him. Jesus cares deeply about this. When Adam and Eve disobeyed God in the garden, the first question that God asked was "Where are you?" It was not "What have you done?" which is the natural thing to ask when you know a grave transgression has occurred. Funny thing is, God already knew where Adam and Eve were. After all, He is God. Yet His main concern was where Adam and Eve were in *relational connection* to Him. It mattered to Him that they were hiding from Him. It mattered to Him that they no longer wholeheartedly trusted Him. Their shame and fear were the consequences of severed intimacy with their Father.

Yes, what you do matters. It matters a lot. However, where your heart is with God matters more. You can begin by considering what draws your focus and attention the most throughout each day. You can even assess your worries, obsessions, and unhealthy desires. Today's a great day to reflect on the position of your heart. Where are you with Jesus today? If you find that you have very little motivation to pray, why do you think that is? What would you rather be doing now? (For example, watching movies, scrolling through social media, or going back to seemingly more productive tasks?) And why? Where have you been in this season of your life? Enjoying friendship with God begins by aligning our hearts with Him.

ACKNOWLEDGE
JESUS

POUR OUT
YOUR HEART

MEDITATE

GENESIS 3:1-13

REFLECT

A general biblical principle you will witness throughout Scripture is that divine friendship with God produces good, which is why cultivating a divine friendship with Him has direct consequences in our lives. Adam and Eve had perfect fellowship with God, and every dysfunction on this earth, past and present, began when that fellowship was broken. It started when the Enemy convinced them not to trust what God had to say about the tree of the knowledge of good and evil (Genesis 3:1-5).

It's important to note here that the Enemy did not have to threaten them. All he had to do was make them doubt God's goodness. Although they were living in abundance and freedom, they began perceiving it as *not good enough*. Even though Adam and Eve lived in the garden and physically remained in God's realm in that moment, their hearts began to depart from Him when they stopped wholeheartedly trusting in His character and intention. Thankfully, Jesus came to restore what was broken in the garden.

You can believe that He is good while simultaneously questioning whether He is good enough, even if you don't realize that is what you're doing. You can go through all the Christian motions without truly trusting Him at all. Are there any matters where you are dissatisfied with God? How would you describe your friendship with Him today?

WEEK  2

RESTORE JOY

God designed you to be the most satisfied when you are *most* in love with Him. A genuine love for Jesus produces harmony between Heavenly Father and child because you will begin to align your thoughts and desires to His. This is the essence of purity—when you find satisfaction in God over all things. Purity is not moral perfection conjured up by immense self-control, nor is it the fruit of undistracted piety. After all, pressure cannot produce purity. Instead, purity is the fruit of loving Jesus with so much devotion that all our other loyalties on earth cannot compare. Anything that threatens this great love has no space.

Consequently, our joy in Him is compromised when other desires *challenge* our love for God. If Christianity is not enjoyable to you, it is likely because there is a rivalry of desires combating within your soul. A want that interrupts our romance with God can be seemingly innocent, such as an obsession with scrolling on your phone. It can consume your thoughts, such as the compulsive need to please people. Or it can be the unbreakable grip of destructive addictions. Although we are welcome to love other people and things, our fealty to them should not prevent us from wholeheartedly living for Christ, or else they could numb us from the pleasures of His Presence.

The essence of purity is love. Yet, if some of us were to be honest, we may admit that we do not want Him as much as we should. Friend of God, if that is also you today, know that condemning your lack of passion is not the answer. Criticizing yourself for your shortage of affection for Jesus can become a distraction as well. Just start with that flicker of spiritual hunger that remains in you, for although it may be faint, it still lives. As dim as it may be, recognize it. Honor your desire to want Him. It may be a whisper in comparison to the clamor of other wants, but it is still a melody that reaches heaven.

ACKNOWLEDGE
JESUS

_____
_____
_____
_____
_____
_____
_____
_____
_____
_____

POUR OUT
YOUR HEART

_____
_____
_____
_____
_____
_____
_____
_____
_____
_____

MEDITATE
PSALM 51

REFLECT

This was King David's prayer after being exposed for his sin. David penned this lament after Nathan the prophet exposed him for wrongfully impregnating Bathsheba and murdering her husband to cover his adultery. It should have never happened. He should have been in battle with his troops. He should have never called for her to meet him in a private place. He shouldn't have tried to hide the consequences by deceitfully placing her husband on the front lines of battle. A few steps away from God led to a chasm. His devotion to his Heavenly Father was divided because he became more loyal to his entitlement, lust, and pride. In response to being made aware of how far he'd fallen from his first love, this was his confession and plea—for God to create in him a clean heart and restore to him the joy of salvation. He didn't present to God any religious regimen for his own restoration, for he knew that striving had no power to change him. Instead, he humbly asked the Creator to create in him the desires and joys that he did not have at that time. Friend of God, what does God need to create in you today? Do you find yourself striving to make up for what you lack spiritually in any way? Do you have competing desires that divide your devotion to God?

PRAY

WEEK  3

ENJOY REDEMPTION

We've all had work friends—and if you haven't, I'm sure you've heard of this kind of friendship. This is the kind of friend that you see and talk to only at work who has very little involvement in your personal life. The same could be said of college friends, church friends, and so on! They are companions with limited influence in your life because you only interact with them in the common space that you share, whether it is school or an office. Sometimes, we treat God in a similar way. Although He is fully present, we limit His impact over us because we do not involve Him. We may acknowledge Him in our worship services and consider Him our moral compass but not regard Him as pertinent to any other day-to-day concerns. We may engage Him at church, but we might not approach the Comforter when we are heartbroken over a relationship. Yet salvation makes Jesus our life friend, the kind that is interested in influencing every inch of our lives.

Friend of God, Christ did not merely pay for your end-of-life ticket to heaven, nor is He only relevant to you when you are involved in religious activities. He is not just interested in your "spiritual life"; the Redeemer is keen on being involved in every part of you—your relationships, your past, your physical health, your finances, and so on. The gift of salvation is restored intimacy with a life-giving Father, making the help of heaven accessible to you in *this very moment*. This is good news. Salvation means you have direct access to the God who is also called Jehovah-jireh (the Lord will provide), Jehovah-rophe (the Lord who heals), and Jehovah-shalom (the Lord is peace). You can involve Him in today's concerns and your immediate needs. He not only saved you for what is to come later in eternity, but He intends to help you, comfort you, and guide you today as well. And tomorrow. And the next day. Thank God for salvation! Let's enjoy it this week.

ACKNOWLEDGE
JESUS

_____
_____
_____
_____
_____
_____
_____
_____
_____

POUR OUT
YOUR HEART

_____
_____
_____
_____
_____
_____
_____
_____
_____

MEDITATE

PSALM 63

REFLECT

It is not exactly clear whether David wrote this psalm while running from King Saul or his son Absalom, for he hid in the wilderness on both occasions. However, what *is* clear is that he needed redemption. He was in dire straits, and he needed more than human help. He needed healing, restoration, provision, and comfort from God Himself. So, David intentionally accessed the divine friendship that he had with his redeemer. Observe all the actions of David as the NIV translation puts it:

- "Earnestly I seek you." (verse 1)
- "My lips will glorify you." (verse 3)
- "I will praise you." (verse 4)
- "On my bed I remember you." (verse 6)
- "I think of you." (verse 6)
- "I sing." (verse 7)
- "I cling to you." (verse 8)

These are the actions of a desperate man who knew that God was the only answer to his needs in the wilderness. David actively invited God to have His way over David's life. Although David was in the wilderness, he was able to access heaven. Regardless of what was around him, he turned his entire being toward God. He fixated on the Presence of God with his thoughts, words, and physical actions. In what ways do you need the Redeemer this week? Into what areas of your life will you intentionally invite Him?

PRAY

WEEK  4

ENJOY HIS FRIENDSHIP

We live in a time that celebrates growth, progress, and achievement. But how much does it take for us to be satisfied where we are at? I remember once getting very caught up in a popular phone game called *Candy Crush*. It's just what it sounds like—a game about crushing candy. And when you do, the screen lights up, the phone vibrates, and you get this rush of dopamine because it feels like you made progress. After a few months of playing this game, it hit me that no amount of progress was enough. The game felt like it never ended, and some rounds were clearly built so that you must pay a fee to gain the tools to win. Honestly, at a certain point, I was wondering if I was playing the game or if the game was playing me! In the mad chase for the next big gain, I ultimately wasn't gaining much at all. Life can feel this way as well—a mad chase for wins, gains, and dopamine rushes. Hustling for peace and happiness is like chasing after the wind.

Someone who understood this mad chase well was King Solomon. His reign was marked by extravagance. Everything he wanted, he attained. Yet, he, too, realized that it was a never-ending and futile pursuit in view of eternity. What makes life significant is not what we gain and attain in our limited time on earth, but rather *who we know*. Our friendship with Jesus in this very moment is the only eternal investment we can make, for the rest fades and proves to be of little importance over time. Salvation allows us to view eternity as a good thing—a great thing, in fact—because it gifts us with a divine friendship that we can enjoy *right now* and *forever*. So, friend of God, what does it take for you to be fully satisfied? Do you ever find yourself chasing after the wind?

ACKNOWLEDGE
JESUS

_____
_____
_____
_____
_____
_____
_____
_____
_____

POUR OUT
YOUR HEART

_____
_____
_____
_____
_____
_____
_____
_____
_____

MEDITATE

ECCLESIASTES 3:9-14

REFLECT

Ecclesiastes begins with Solomon's lament over the triviality of all things "under the sun." He essentially peeked at life and found nothing of everlasting value. He confessed in Ecclesiastes 1:8, "All things are wearisome, more than anyone can say. The eye is not satisfied by seeing or the ear filled with hearing." His tune changed only when he meditated on how vast, great, and forever God is. When he considered forever, he realized that *the very moment he lived in* was a gift from God. As he recognized just how limited and fleeting his life was, he realized that the wisest thing to do was to enjoy the gift of "now." You do not have to wait to accomplish that goal or build that ideal family to be considered blessed. Every blessing that matters is already yours in Christ. Why not rejoice today? Why not be thankful for each breath? Why not appreciate all that God has done rather than pining for the things that haven't transpired yet?

PRAY

WEEK  5

JESUS UNDERSTANDS

God isn't just with you, He fully understands you as well. Imagine that, friend! He isn't apathetically looming like a glorified Elf on a Shelf toy. He isn't an indifferent witness to every thought and action that comes out of you. Rather, He gets your struggle. His empathy is not charity because it is from personal experience. As a youth pastor, I interacted with many parents of my students over the years. I would sit with them as they wept in worry over their children or asked for extra prayers. I felt for them at that time, but I did not understand them. It wasn't until I had children of my own that I understood their urgency. My experience with parents drastically changed when I became a parent myself. They had my heart as they were concerned about their children getting bullied. They had my tears when their children were struggling. I was in touch with them in a deeper way because I understood them. Just as Jesus understands us.

Although Jesus is God, He came to us as a man, with all the limitations of humanity. When you survey His life in the Gospels, you will observe a wide array of emotions and human experiences. He felt them all. He knows what it feels like to be tired, misunderstood, abandoned, tempted, and angry in this fallen world. He chose to humble Himself to that level of closeness with us. Christ's incarnation from heaven to earth was an extravagant demonstration of love. Quite frankly, I love my dogs and am with them often, but I won't ever fully understand their experience because I would never choose to live as one of them! Jesus ensured that there was no separation like this between us. It takes a radical amount of affection and commitment to do what Christ did. He chose to immerse Himself into our world and now our strife—personally.

ACKNOWLEDGE
JESUS

POUR OUT
YOUR HEART

MEDITATE

ISAIAH 53:1-6

REFLECT

Isaiah 53 recounts Christ's incarnational ministry from His life on earth to His death and resurrection. It starts with this question: "And to whom has the arm of the Lord been revealed?" "The arm of the Lord" refers to God's great power, and that great power was revealed through the ordinary humanity He chose to live with while on earth. As you consider how our omniscient King chose to present Himself in such humble form, how does it shape your perspective of Christ? He was entitled to live as the perfect and almighty God that He is. He could have even come as a rich and powerful man. Yet, from the start of His time on earth, He chose to embrace all the vulnerability and fragility of humanity. A baby cradled in the arms of a weary young mother (Luke 2). A man who knew the torture of temptation (Matthew 4:1). A tired sojourner who had to rest by a well to quench His thirst (John 4:5–6). A tearful mourner (John 11:35). A troubled soul who was overwhelmed to the point of death (Matthew 26:37–39). Jesus chose to live as humans live and endure what the guilty deserved. He gets pain. He understands limitations. And His great empathy overflows to us. Can we appreciate this for a moment? Can you imagine being a recipient of such kindness and compassion?

PRAY

WEEK  6

CHAMPIONED BY GRACE

Around the time of my first book release, I was in the car with a dear friend of mine, and we were casually chatting about this monumental day that was approaching. All of a sudden, she interrupted our conversation and shouted, "You need a cake!" With sheer enthusiasm, she got wide-eyed and started rapidly questioning whether I was having a book party, whether I was "celebrating this moment," and so on—to which I sheepishly replied, "No." Within five minutes, she rallied up our closest friends to arrange for everyone to make time and fly out to where I lived. We were going to have a party—with cake, of course. I did not know how to receive this amount of unearned support, so I sat there in silence with this wave of love crashing toward me. It wasn't just because of the cake, although the cake sounded fantastic. It was that she cared about my wins. My victories were hers to celebrate as well. She saw into me and was *for me.* It uplifted me to my core. There's nothing like that feeling of truly being championed by someone.

As sweet as this moment was, it doesn't even compare to the force of God's love that is *for* you this week. As soon as you yield your life to Jesus, *you are His* to protect and bless. Grace ensures that He remains on your team no matter how hard you fall. God is your ultimate champion. He always planned to be, even before you knew Him. And because of His saving grace, He always will be, even after your greatest blunders. He cares deeply about what you are facing today and wants to be involved. When was the last time you knew and felt that God was your champion?

ACKNOWLEDGE
JESUS

_____
_____
_____
_____
_____
_____
_____
_____
_____
_____

POUR OUT
YOUR HEART

_____
_____
_____
_____
_____
_____
_____
_____
_____
_____

MEDITATE
ZEPHANIAH 3:9–17

REFLECT

Zephaniah was a prophet during the reign of King Josiah, and he urgently warned the people of Judah to repent and seek the Lord because God's judgment of their sins was near. Although he intricately described God's impending wrath, it was not without the promise of God's restoration. Ultimately, God's intention was not to leave His people in ruin, but rather to save them. Just as a parent would scream for a child who is walking toward danger, the forcefulness of Zephaniah's words echoed the heart of a God who cares deeply for what becomes of His people. He is a passionate Father, mighty to save and defend not those who have earned His favor, but rather those who are willing to be His children. Because what Jesus did on the cross was so thorough, He remains your friend and champion even when you are at your worst. Are there any ways that you may need a Divine Champion today?

PRAY

WEEK  7

JESUS IS LORD

Friend of God, I'm glad you're here today. Despite everything that is calling your name for attention, you have chosen to lean into Jesus in this hour. I celebrate this with you. No matter what demand, obligation, or job you have before you, our ultimate purpose will always be to take pleasure in the growing divine friendship that's been given to us by grace. Interrupting the day to enjoy His Presence is a triumph of this very purpose, a declaration that you are no longer the master of your life because you have surrendered the reins to your savior.

Jesus Christ is Lord. But He is also Lord *over our lives.* We can recognize the first statement without surrendering to the latter. If you are constantly stressed and anxious, perhaps it is because you are still desperately trying to be the builder and protector of your own destiny. Instead of living as dependent children of a good Father, we may be trying to be the independent master of our universe, a role we were not designed to play. We offer our lives in prayer, but once the prayer is done, we may be quick to take back the reins and cling to control, leaving no room for the power of the Holy Spirit to do the things that only He can do. This week, there may be something that you must let go of. It may be the outcome of your infertility journey. Perhaps it's the incessant fear of people's perception of you at work. It could be the growth of your church. If you have embraced Jesus Christ as your Lord, then all your goals and aspirations are surrendered at His feet. Because at the end of the day, you live for Jesus, and your life is His to bless and protect.

ACKNOWLEDGE
JESUS

_____
_____
_____
_____
_____
_____
_____
_____
_____
_____

POUR OUT
YOUR HEART

_____
_____
_____
_____
_____
_____
_____
_____
_____
_____

MEDITATE
MATTHEW 16:24-28

REFLECT

Jesus lays out the foundation of what it takes to be a true disciple, and it is a weighty calling with an even weightier promise. He teaches it clearly: Deny yourself, take up your cross, and follow Him. Many are drawn to Christ for the gains, but to be a disciple, we must also be willing to lose. The imagery of taking up the cross is strong, for it symbolizes an excruciating and humiliating execution. Being a disciple is not just about having an extracurricular religious activity on the weekend. Rather, it is a death to our rights, our entitlements, and even our goals—a radical surrender. Instead of aspiring to live like our favorite Instagram influencer, we are called to live like our Messiah. Instead of following the pressures of societal standards, we are to follow His guidance written in Scripture. Surrendering your life to Him may feel like a great loss at first, especially as you relinquish your rights—the right to dictate and control your life, the right to gain what you feel entitled to. Yet as you allow the grip on your fate to loosen, Jesus promises that you will then find true life. What does taking up your cross look like for you this week? Is there any part of you that may be hesitant to fully surrender, fearing that the promise of true life may not be worth it? There is much grace to reveal those fears to our Good Friend today.

WEEK  8

BEHOLD THE RESURRECTION

Let's pause and take a moment to consider and appreciate the gift of Christ's resurrection this week. It was more than just one of Christ's many miracles because it was the miracle that changed everything. It revealed the insurmountable power of God, the divinity of Christ, the veracity of all that Jesus had said, a hope for more than this life, and so much more. Christ's resurrection is the triumph that made friendship with God possible. It is a powerful reality, but are you personally affected by it? It can be easy to limit our friendship with God to church traditions and inspirational quotes without ever submitting ourselves to the transformative truth of His resurrection. When Christ resurrected, He eradicated every barrier to intimate connection and unconditional friendship with God. When you intentionally appreciate this victory, it enriches the way you enjoy your friendship with Him.

I was present when my husband (at that time a very good "friend") accepted Jesus as his Lord and Savior. He was a college freshman, and we had been in a college small group together for about seven months. For those seven months I thought he was a Christian. I mean, he sure looked like a Christian! He went to every prayer meeting and Bible study. He even volunteered at church. But I will never forget that one fateful Easter morning service. This nineteen-year-old freshman, awkwardly clad in his father's gray suit and blue tie, silently held the communion cup and the piece of bread in his hands. And he wept. I kept hearing him whisper, "Thank You. Thank You." Later he told me that, for the first time, it dawned on him that Jesus died and rose again *for him.* He had always embraced the traditions, but he had never allowed the truth to sink in. He gained a Great Friend that day and has been walking with Him ever since. Perhaps we, too, can use a fresh reminder of what Jesus won for us on that cross. Let's let it sink in and transform us again and again.

ACKNOWLEDGE
JESUS

_____
_____
_____
_____
_____
_____
_____
_____
_____
_____

POUR OUT
YOUR HEART

_____
_____
_____
_____
_____
_____
_____
_____
_____
_____

MEDITATE
MATTHEW 28:1-9

REFLECT

Jesus foretold His crucifixion and resurrection multiple times (for example, Matthew 16:21; 17:22–23; 20:17–19). However, it is one thing to hear the resurrection being foretold, and it is another to believe it in the face of tragedy. The women who visited His tomb weren't looking for good news. Instead, they were planning to go and sit with disappointment in the flesh—a crucified Jesus. To them, the resurrection was an untested hope foretold by their dead teacher. More real to them were the agonizing memories of His body mercilessly hung with nails. In a similar sense, you, too, may be familiar with the details around Christ's resurrection. You may have studied it and even celebrated it at church many times. Yet, disappointment will reveal what you truly believe. The empty tomb and the angel with good news became proof that Jesus defeated bad endings. Great joy erupted in the women who beheld the reality of Christ's resurrection. No matter what this week holds, great joy awaits you in the end, too, my friend. How can your reflection on the resurrection shift your perspective and attitude this week?

PRAY

WEEK  9

REMEMBER THE MAIN THING

Years ago, I had a dream that made a lasting impact on me. In my dream, I was at my wedding. I was cheerfully busy all day with various details. I fiddled around and got my beautiful dress tailored. I also had to talk to the wedding band about practice. The guests were coming in, and I took the time to catch up with some. Hours passed by, and I realized at the end of the day that I had *completely forgotten to invite the groom.* And then I woke up. I was so caught up with the wedding day that I missed the point of the wedding entirely (thank goodness this was just a dream!). Surely, all these things make the festivities of a union sweet, but they are pointless without the union itself. It reminded me of what we so often do as Christians—we get caught up with the blessings of God and forget to invite God Himself.

There are many reasons to follow Jesus other than Jesus Himself. One can even argue that there were varying motivations among the twelve disciples! Pursuing Christianity as a religion has its gains, for it offers a sense of destiny, identity, encouragement, worth, and spiritual community. These are all God's blessings, and just one of these can be desirable enough to motivate our Sunday church attendance. However, Jesus calls us not to settle for anything less than the true gift of the gospel, which is a blood-bought friendship with God. The others are good, but friendship with Him is better. Otherwise, we settle for the shadows of His Presence, often wondering why we are still pining for more. Is friendship with Him something you have chosen to appreciate lately?

ACKNOWLEDGE
JESUS

_____
_____
_____
_____
_____
_____
_____
_____
_____
_____
_____

POUR OUT
YOUR HEART

_____
_____
_____
_____
_____
_____
_____
_____
_____
_____
_____

MEDITATE

LUKE 10:17-20

REFLECT

Jesus appointed seventy-two to go in pairs to evangelize the towns. They were called to go completely by faith, without provision or security measures. In every town they went to, they were to preach the good news and heal the sick. Today's passage describes their victorious march back after they had experienced God's great power and good works. They came back feeling triumphant, full of authority and confidence. This can be mistaken as the apex of our spiritual growth. Yet, Jesus warns them not to relish in this, for the point of salvation is not just to give us power. Luke says in verse 17 that the disciples returned *with joy* because the demons submitted to them! Yet Jesus calls them to rejoice in the better thing: that they were saved and had a relationship with the Father. Friend of God, it is good to enjoy and appreciate the blessings of God. However, let us not forget to enjoy the better thing: our friendship with Him. Perhaps you can take time to adore and worship Him before you make your requests this week. If you find this challenging, you can choose to appreciate the very thing Jesus taught the disciples to rejoice over, and you can do so by praying this prayer: *Jesus, thank You that my name is written in heaven.*

WEEK  10

THE POWER OF CELEBRATION

I have a mission for you this week! Now, before you roll your eyes or close this book, know that this is an important practice for anyone who wants to enjoy friendship with God. The mission is to *celebrate*. Celebration can be a reaction or a choice. We can cheer in reaction to college acceptance letters or after receiving some great news. We can also intentionally choose to celebrate the things that we deem deeply valuable, such as a hard-earned wedding anniversary or a year of sobriety. We can also celebrate our salvation.

Lately, I have found myself grumbling, particularly about my home. I have griped over the repairs that are required or the space that is needed as our children grow bigger and more energetic. I've even gazed longingly at other homes in the neighborhood. In a way, I felt like that's what I needed in order to be "blessed." However, the Lord gently reminded me how, at one point in time, this house was an absolute miracle from God. Years ago, it would have been impossible to move into a home like this, but God did it, and I celebrated that for a long time. Unfortunately, that marveling eventually wore off. But these days, I am choosing to celebrate my home and reconnect with the way God provided.

Celebration is proof that we recognize the worth of what He's given us. Honoring what Jesus has done for us awakens our tired and weary bones to His Presence. It activates our sleepy senses, tuning them in to heavenly hope. Salvation was a costly gift, and celebrating it ensures that we honor that gift.

ACKNOWLEDGE
JESUS

_____
_____
_____
_____
_____
_____
_____
_____
_____
_____

POUR OUT
YOUR HEART

_____
_____
_____
_____
_____
_____
_____
_____
_____
_____

MEDITATE

LUKE 15:22-32

REFLECT

The father keeps encouraging celebration. Why? No one achieved anything substantial. There was no great win to commemorate— other than the fact that his younger son returned. No one recognized this more than the elder brother. Out of jealousy and spite, he *refused* to celebrate. But the father did not stand for it. The matter of celebration was so important that the master of the household was willing to pursue and plead with the one who refused to join the festivities. He reminded the elder brother that he, too, must rejoice because he always had all the benefits of being his father's son. The elder son could not celebrate the restoration of his brother because *he had forgotten the blessings and privileges of the relationship that he himself had all along.* Celebrating what God has done and who God is awakens your senses to experience the goodness of His friendship. It is a recognition of worth. It is intentional enjoyment. How will you celebrate God's blessings this week?

WEEK  11

YOUR INVITATION MATTERS

God is everywhere. This is true. However, God is not *invited* every-where. After living in our home for a year, my husband decided to invite some husbands in the neighborhood over for fellowship. It was going to be a casual night with the neighbors outside on the porch on a cool fall evening. One of the neighbors nervously came with his hands full of gifts, something that no one really anticipated or asked for. It turned out that he had been living in America for around thirty years, but no one had ever invited him into their home before. Our jaws dropped! We had been living by this man and his family, waving at each other, and borrowing tools for a year. But everything changed with one invitation. It allowed us to enjoy new levels of friendship with one another.

We honor those we invite into our more personal spaces. When we invite the Holy Spirit, we honor Him as well. He may be welcomed into moments like this when you take time out for a good ol' devotional, but is He invited into your relationships? Is He invited into your thought life? How about your plans for the future? The difference between inviting a neighbor and inviting God is that God is *King.* When we invite Him, we also make room for His rule and reign. We answer to Him because His dominion brings freedom. We welcome His wisdom to establish peace. We acknowledge Him with worship, and in doing so, we trade darkness for light. Everything changes when we intentionally invite the Holy Spirit to direct our lives. This opens the door to deeper levels of friendship with Him.

ACKNOWLEDGE
JESUS

_____
_____
_____
_____
_____
_____
_____
_____
_____
_____

POUR OUT
YOUR HEART

_____
_____
_____
_____
_____
_____
_____
_____
_____
_____

MEDITATE

ACTS 8:4-8

REFLECT

Stephen was the first martyr for the gospel, and an outbreak of severe persecution followed his death. The church scattered in the aftermath of his murder. Yet evil did not affect God's plans because it was from there the church went beyond Jerusalem and carried the good news to the nations. Whenever Christ's followers preached the good news, people welcomed the Holy Spirit, and He defended the gospel with signs and miracles. Philip may have run from Jerusalem, but he had authority over evil because he had the Presence of God with him. Philip invited God wherever he went. When he preached, the crowds did not stone him. They paid attention and believed the message. Consequently, they, too, learned to invite God, and this changed their city. Darkness could not prevail where Jesus was welcomed. And great joy ensued. Friend of God, if you want to experience more of Him, you must offer more of yourself. Invite Him to speak to you when you are eating your meals alone. Ask Him for guidance when you are dealing with family conflict. Acknowledge Him wherever you are. In what ways can you intentionally invite the Holy Spirit into the spaces in your life?

WEEK  12

BELIEVE BEFORE YOU FEEL

What if you cannot feel God? Friend, I've been there more times than I can count. It can feel like you have failed when you aren't perpetually on cloud nine with Jesus. You know you should pray, but you keep binge-watching television shows instead. You know the power of worship, but you don't have a song in you to sing. And although you want to be happy for those who gush about their connection to Jesus, it can also pressure you at the same time. How can you experience friendship with God if you are not really feeling anything?

What you feel has nothing to do with where He is and what He is doing. Imagine holding other relationships in our lives to the same expectations that we hold God to. If I told my friends I would doubt our friendship each time a day went by without our exchanging a text message, that would be unfair to them. If I told my spouse that I doubted the reality of our marriage because I do not feel the butterflies anymore when he is around, that would be an impossible demand to place on him. Yet, we do it to God all the time! When our prayers are met with stillness, we can misinterpret silence as abandonment. If we are not emotionally moved after a Bible reading, we can question whether God is doing anything at all. In doing so, we allow our experience to determine the quality of the covenant that Christ had paid for. Friend of God, He bled to remain with you always. We must allow God's covenant with us to determine how we feel about our relationship with Him instead of letting our temporary feelings affect our view of His covenant.

ACKNOWLEDGE
JESUS

POUR OUT
YOUR HEART

MEDITATE
ROMANS 8:31-39

REFLECT

God never promises a painless life. Instead, He promises a victorious one. Those who accept the gift of salvation are no longer destined to merely survive. No more striving to remain in His good graces. No more looking for worth from the things and people on earth. No more fear of death. No more worrying about our lot. No more hopelessness. No more shame. Jesus has *removed everything that could have disqualified you* from being fully His. You cannot lose what you were never able to earn in the first place. Note here that Romans says that God is for *you* and not necessarily your current expectations and agendas. This is not a passage that we can conveniently use for positive vibes toward whatever we want, but it does endow us with a supernatural confidence, assuring us that we never endure trials alone. You are not just a survivor of circumstance. You are not a broken consequence of your past. You are not a failure who is merely tolerated by God. You are *more than a conqueror.* The NLT version of this phrase is "overwhelming victory is ours through Christ" (verse 37). Let's bask in that, friend. Even if the feelings are not there yet, in what ways can you live by this immutable truth this week?

PRAY

WEEK  13

LETTING GO OF REGRET

Let's deal with regret. We all know this feeling, and it can block us from fully enjoying God's Presence. To clarify, I don't mean the healthy, sensible kind of regret that can offer helpful lessons and growth. The regret I speak of is the kind that you cannot get over, the kind that plagues your soul. Have you ever struggled with it? It keeps you stuck in the past and paralyzed with shame. Sometimes we attempt to ignore regret by trying harder to make up for what we cannot forgive ourselves for. Regret feels like a tiresome striving when we are constantly seeking to compensate for what we cannot undo. For others, regret is the torment of self-hatred and compulsive guilt. We hold on to it because we feel like we deserve it.

The difficulty with regret is that it can feel like a holy burden, as if it is something righteous to cling to. In a way, it feels like we are paying penance for our wrongs. But this isn't the will of God for us, for holding on to regret is a denial of God's grace. We cannot freely commune with the Holy Spirit unless we humbly embrace forgiveness and accept unconditional love. It's awkward to receive at times, especially for those of us who feel the need to prove our worthiness. Our value cannot be earned; rather, it must be freely received. Grace like this can make one nervous because it seems too good to be true. But that is why the gospel is good news.

Friend of God, today is a great day to be free of any age-old regrets. You can ask the Holy Spirit to reveal the regrets that you have ignored for some time. You are safe to bring up untold secrets and the shame buried in your past. He does not meet your confessions with a whip. He is unconditional love and your most loyal Friend. The blood of Jesus saved you at the moment of your redemption, and it will continue to save you for the rest of your days.

ACKNOWLEDGE
JESUS

POUR OUT
YOUR HEART

MEDITATE

2 CORINTHIANS 7:8–13

REFLECT

The apostle Paul was a spiritual father to the Corinthian church. He sent them the letter of 2 Corinthians to guide and correct them in their spiritual journey. In this particular letter, he references a previous letter that harshly rebuked the congregation. Although it brought them grief, Paul rejoiced because it instilled in them a godly grief and not a worldly one. The difference between godly grief and worldly grief is that godly grief is a response to God's kindness and mercy. It dawns on us as we realize what we have done and just how much He loves us still. When in this place, we want to change because of love. The relief of forgiveness invigorates us to try again. Worldly grief, however, entangles us in deep regret. It denies grace and rejects God's kindness. Worldly grief does not glorify God because it upholds our sins higher than His love. You honor Christ more by receiving His forgiveness and moving forward than by denying grace and remaining in torment. If you find yourself carrying this sort of regret today, can you confess it through prayer and leave it at the feet of Jesus?

PRAY

WEEK  14

GROW IN UNDERSTANDING

Do you know that it is possible to *be* blessed and still not *feel* blessed? Even the best gifts cannot be properly enjoyed unless we recognize their worth. For example, an expensive car wouldn't mean much to a toddler, but their ability to be dazzled by the gift would grow as their understanding grows. Similarly, the beauty in salvation is meant to get better over time. The start of your faith is not meant to be the height of your spiritual experience. Although that sacred beginning may be electric with excitement and newness, you grow in spiritual insight over time. The more you grow in insight, the more you enjoy His Presence. Salvation is like a gift that you are continuously unwrapping and unveiling by faith.

When I moved into my current home, I hardly had time to appreciate what was going on during the first week of transition. It was in the middle of 2020, and to find a house in northern New Jersey at that time was quite the feat. We found a place in the nick of time (praise the Lord!), and we were in over our heads with boxes, cleaning, and unpacking. Quite frankly, I was just glad to have a place to go to. It wasn't until a month later that I started to recognize details in the house that I had never noticed before. There was a beautiful little stream behind the trees in our backyard, so the sound of water was always present in the background. The driveway was long enough for our children to spend the day making the most elaborate chalk murals. Our living room was large enough to hold Bible studies with our church members. In the rush of the move, I hadn't recognized these details of the home. But once I did, my heart exploded with gratitude and pleasure. This is a mere portrait of what our experience with Jesus is meant to be like. You may have a few great memories with Him already, but there is so much more for you.

ACKNOWLEDGE
JESUS

_____
_____
_____
_____
_____
_____
_____
_____
_____
_____

POUR OUT
YOUR HEART

_____
_____
_____
_____
_____
_____
_____
_____
_____
_____

MEDITATE

EPHESIANS 1:15-19

REFLECT

The apostle Paul addressed this letter to the Christians of Ephesus. Even though they were already followers of Jesus, Paul prayed that they would receive *more* wisdom and revelation in the knowledge of God. He did not pray that they would merely "feel" more. Instead, he prayed that their personal knowledge of what God had already given them would expand and deepen. You may already know that you are saved in Christ, but you may not be experiencing hope and power because you need fresh conviction and insight. Even though the Ephesians were believers, they still needed more of this. How does the apostle Paul address this need? He prayed for the Ephesians. He asked God to give them the spiritual insight needed to experience hope, His glorious inheritance, and the greatness of His power. You can pray this prayer for yourself as well! If you need the joy of your salvation restored or rejuvenated, I invite you to pray this prayer: *Holy Spirit, please enlighten the eyes of my heart so that I may know the hope of Your calling, the wealth of Your glorious inheritance, and the greatness of Your power toward me.*

WEEK  15

SUPERNATURAL ONENESS

God wants you. Yes, *you*, dear reader. The condition of your heart right now may be nothing to be proud of. The quality of your character may need some work. Yet, just as you are here because you want Him, know that He wants you too. *Atonement* is a big word that means God paid a high price so He doesn't have to spend eternity without you. *Eerdmans Bible Dictionary* describes *atonement* as a "human reunion with God through Christ."[1] It's not just a clean slate that is charitably offered by a great God to a helpless and decrepit humankind. Atonement is a supernatural *oneness* made possible by a humble Father. Genesis 1–2 displays God's loving intention for humankind. Then in Genesis 3 through the end of Revelation, the Bible records His tireless pursuit of our souls. We are atoned for because He is love, and our broken promises and selfish motives cannot make Him any less Himself. Atonement doesn't deal with God by making Him kinder to us. Rather, it deals with us.

Have you ever felt the immense relief of being forgiven? Every conscience-stricken soul is welcome to approach Jesus and feast on grace. Repentance is a means to enjoy God's atonement for us. It allows us to experience this supernatural oneness that Jesus paid for. Repentance requires vulnerability with the Holy Spirit. We must be willing to admit to our self-absorbed desires and unveil the most shameful nooks and crannies of our minds. This may call for some introspection because some sins are easier to point out than others. Ask the Holy Spirit to guide you in this. But know that the work of repentance is not just developing self-awareness. That won't lead you to freedom. Ultimately, repentance must also lead you to an awareness of grace, and you must receive God's forgiveness in order to enjoy it.

ACKNOWLEDGE

JESUS

_____
_____
_____
_____
_____
_____
_____
_____
_____
_____

POUR OUT

YOUR HEART

_____
_____
_____
_____
_____
_____
_____
_____
_____
_____

MEDITATE

1 JOHN 1:5-2:2

REFLECT

The proof of genuine intimacy with the Holy Spirit will be in the transformation of our lives. If you befriend the light, you will live in light. Verse 6 admonishes us not to deceive others by feigning religiosity without choosing to live according to God's ways. Verse 8, on the other hand, admonishes us not to deceive ourselves by living as if we do not fall short of the glory of God. Let's be honest—with God, with others, and with ourselves. How do we remain honest? By making repentance a regular practice. There will always be a need to repent while we are living this life. This doesn't need to discourage us because Jesus is our friend and advocate. He is eager to defend you. After all, He was the One who made a way for atonement, for that oneness with you. You can begin by asking the Holy Spirit to reveal to you the motives, mindsets, and actions that fall short of His glory. Is there anything that comes up? After you confess to Him and embrace His grace, what are some steps you can take to turn your words into action as well?

WEEK  16

CONSIDER ETERNITY

Friend of God, this week I want us to give thought to eternity. Go ahead and take a pause right here to imagine it. Go past decades from now. Go even farther and think about the time beyond your lifetime. Keep going until you can imagine your forever with Jesus. Everyone is immortal and will spend eternity somewhere. Our limited time on this side of heaven is a brief opportunity to make an imperishable investment for our endless future. Yes, today has its share of pressures. Tomorrow may loom over you with threats of what's to come. But eternity is imminent. We cannot afford to forget that we are eternal beings.

Thankfully, our salvation in Christ allows us to look forward to eternity and not dread it. Salvation means that what awaits us is perfect communion with our Father in heaven and a city that is so glorious it doesn't even need the sun to shine upon it (Revelation 21:23). The painful memories of our time on this earth will not even cast a shadow into our forever. This perpetuity of time should be the filter through which you see everything and everyone. Every time you get a check, meet a person, or tackle a problem, ask yourself how you could handle this in a way that would have the deepest, most positive impact in heaven. You will find that most things you spend your energy on will not matter even five years from now, let alone fifty years or one thousand years from now. Remember, you will keep going after your lifetime, and your current frustrations will not go with you.

ACKNOWLEDGE
JESUS

POUR OUT
YOUR HEART

MEDITATE

REVELATION 21:1-8

REFLECT

The apostle John received these visions while imprisoned on the island of Patmos. Such a peek into what is to come must have strengthened him to persevere in the face of persecution. He saw a vision of what will transpire after the final judgment, after unbelievers are cast into an eternity of punishment (Revelation 20:10, 15). All things will be made new. What makes this new city heaven is that God will freely dwell with His people, just as it was meant to be. There will be no lack nor dissatisfaction. There will be no pining for more because we will drink from the spring of life (Revelation 21:6). While Christians today have a regenerated spirit, we still live in a fallen world. One day, the world will also be regenerated. We will be home at last. God wanted John to remember eternity. Although he was wrapped in darkness while in exile, he would one day be basking in the glory of God's Presence with the entire family of believers. Sweet communion with Jesus will be an everyday reality, while all pain will be but a faint memory. Can you envision that, friend?

PRAY

ENJOYING

HIS

PRESENCE

WEEK  17

WHAT DO YOU THINK OF GOD?

If you desire to grow in your enjoyment of God's Presence, you must consider how you think of Him. The key to growing in enjoyment of Him is not accruing more emotional events or mystical encounters. It begins with trusting Jesus, and that trust is rooted in a commitment to the gospel truth. Friend of God, you must first remember that He is good. You must know His goodness intimately so that this conviction can shape how you feel, especially during difficult seasons.

God is not an energy force to lure with our good deeds. He is not someone to use for a better life; He is someone to *know*. And how we know Him will determine how we experience Him. If we believe that He is distant and disconnected, we will hesitate to run to Him when we are vulnerable. If we believe that He is a cruel teacher, we will immediately feel condemnation and shame after every mistake. What we think of God matters!

If you are not sure what you genuinely think of Him, consider how you react to Him when you are enduring pain. Pain reveals our most candid perspective of God. It's easier to acknowledge that He is almighty and powerful on a cerebral level. You can even sing about it at church. Nevertheless, your response to dire need and grave disappointment reveals what you think of Him at a heart level. This is why wilderness seasons shake us to the core. Difficulty doesn't atrophy our belief; it actually reveals the limitations to our belief—which is a gift. If pain exposes our innermost opinion of God, then it makes our friendship with Him more honest. We may not have asked for this unveiling, but we can definitely use it to return to the truth of who God is.

ACKNOWLEDGE
JESUS

_____
_____
_____
_____
_____
_____
_____
_____
_____
_____

POUR OUT
YOUR HEART

_____
_____
_____
_____
_____
_____
_____
_____
_____

MEDITATE

GENESIS 2:8-18

REFLECT

Genesis 1–2 reveals God's intention for the world because it records how He set things up according to His perfect design. Everything that grew was pleasing. The garden was abundant with provision. It wasn't a place to survive; it was a place to thrive. And when God placed Adam in the garden, He gave him both direction and admonition to *freely enjoy* this paradise. His commands began with, "You are free." And although it came with a directive not to eat from the tree of the knowledge of good and evil, the heart of the Father was to set His child up to *flourish*. This early picture of existence exudes God's goodness. We know later in Genesis 3 that the Enemy comes and immediately twists God's words and casts a negative light on His character by saying, "Did God really say, 'You can't eat from any tree in the garden'?" (Genesis 3:1). Isn't it profound how you can be in paradise and still be dissatisfied with your friendship with God? The serpent simply convinced Adam and Eve to shift how they thought of Him. They no longer trusted His judgment, so they turned to another pleasure and tried to make their own way to joy. The rest is history. What you think of Him matters. Let's dig into the layers of your internal belief system and see if there are any false beliefs or negative opinions of Him. You may find yourself having thoughts like, "I should think _____, but I actually think _____," or "I know He is _____, but it feels like He isn't." Experience God's goodness by bringing these thoughts to the Holy Spirit and trusting that He will meet you with grace.

WEEK  18

THE GIFT OF YOUR ATTENTION

The currency of today's culture is your attention. Businesses spend an exorbitant amount on branding and marketing to grab your attention and keep it. Driving down the highway, you can see larger-than-life billboards designed to capture your gaze. On social media, you are bombarded by carefully crafted imagery and captions intended to captivate you, enticing you to linger a little longer or click. Your attention is valuable. We exalt and magnify what we focus on, which is why giving the Presence of God our attention is so important. It isn't just for Him but for us as well. When we shift our internal gaze toward heaven, we position ourselves to hear from Him and receive His help. When you acknowledge Him, you make yourself accessible to Him and allow Him to touch you in supernatural ways.

When Peter's attention was on Jesus, he walked on water. Then his attention went to the winds, and he sank (Matthew 14:28–30). When the Canaanite woman needed deliverance for her demon-possessed daughter, she cried out to Jesus. She refused to be distracted. Even upon dismissal, she knelt before Him. She kept her attention fixed on Jesus instead of being swayed by the negative noise around her. In response to her faith and focus, Jesus performed a miracle and healed her daughter (Matthew 15:21–28). Friend of God, where is your attention today?

ACKNOWLEDGE
JESUS

_____
_____
_____
_____
_____
_____
_____
_____
_____

POUR OUT
YOUR HEART

_____
_____
_____
_____
_____
_____
_____
_____
_____

MEDITATE

EXODUS 33:7-11

REFLECT

Most people could not approach God like Moses and Joshua did. It was a sacred thing for a mere man to enter the tent to interact with the Divine as a friend. It was such a wonder that all the people honored the meeting by standing at their own tents and bowing in worship while the cloud of God's Presence remained at the entrance of the meeting place. An even greater wonder is our access to the Holy Spirit. Thanks to the atonement of Christ, we ourselves are the tent of meeting, and we can commune with God as a friend as well. Joshua understood the value of this wonder and lingered with the Presence of God. Even when Moses returned to the camp to tend to his duties, Joshua chose to remain. He could have been far more productive outside the tent. Yet, this was his preparation for becoming Israel's next leader. He had to be a friend of God first. How? By offering a sacrifice of time and attention. By dwelling with God for a time, Joshua was marked forever. We are shaped and influenced by what we give our attention to. Enjoying God's Presence and friendship does not need to be complicated. You just need to offer Him the gift of your attention.

PRAY

WEEK  19

HE DWELLS WITH YOU

Friend of God, here's a truth to remember today: The glory of God is within you. Listen . . . I do not mean this figuratively! I very much mean this literally! This may seem like an overstatement, especially if your current situation feels mundane at best. You may not be feeling like a carrier of God's glory. Yet, as a Christian, you must take this to heart. It is not a fluffy platitude to inspire you for the day. If Jesus is your Lord and Savior, then the glory of God dwells within you (1 Corinthians 6:19–20).

The glory of God is His manifest Presence, a visible expression of His holiness and magnificence. In the Old Testament, the glory of God had dwellings where He resided in proximity to the Israelites. This was necessary because He was a perfectly holy God who loved a fallen and sinful people. To dwell with the Israelites, there needed to be boundaries, sacrifices, and procedures. At first, His glory appeared in the tabernacle that Moses set up (Exodus 40:34–35). Later, His glory filled the temple that King Solomon built (2 Chronicles 7:1). Then, because of the Israelites' sins, the glory of God departed (Ezekiel 11:22–23), only to later dwell among humankind again with the arrival of Jesus Christ (John 1:14). And now the glory of God resides within us as the Holy Spirit (John 17:22). Friend of God, you are the tabernacle. You are the temple. And He will not leave you as He did the Israelites, no matter what the state of your heart is today. No matter what grade you give yourself as a Christian, what was once covered in a veil shines through you.

ACKNOWLEDGE
JESUS

POUR OUT
YOUR HEART

MEDITATE
LEVITICUS 9:15-24

REFLECT

After establishing the priestly ministry, Aaron and Moses were able to present to a holy God an offering on behalf of the people's sins. Then the glory of God appeared before the Israelites and consumed the offering with fire. This was a sign that God accepted their sacrifices and, therefore, accepted the people. The miracle was not just in the fire but in the gracious acceptance that came from the Almighty. Their response afterward was not coerced by tradition or religious pressure. It was a genuine reaction of joy and reverence. The word "shouted" in this passage is the Hebrew word *ranan,* which is to "shout for joy."[1] Upon experiencing God's acceptance and witnessing His glory, they burst into shouts and prostrated themselves in humility. It was both a wonder and honor for Yahweh to be willing to dwell among a sinful people. For us, we can witness that same glorious acceptance *every time* we consider the cross—the place where the Lamb of God was offered so that we may be embraced by our Father. It is still a gracious miracle and an honor, worthy of shouts of joy and reverence. What are some ways you can express your appreciation of His gracious nearness and acceptance this week?

PRAY

WEEK  20

DON'T WAIT TO LOVE HIM

Once when I was struggling with my faith, I sat in a dimly lit auditorium and watched an evangelist's eyes water as he talked adoringly about Jesus. I envied what he had. I wondered why God would show up for Him in such a real and tangible way while leaving me with what felt like empty prayers. I wanted that closeness for myself. When you feel bad for your lack of spiritual passion, you can pressure yourself into conjuring feelings of being in good standing with God. But there is no prerequisite to loving on Jesus. Your devotion to Him need not wait for a rush of sentiment. It can be freely given to the One we find worthy. Brother Lawrence said,

> People seek for methods of learning to love God. They hope to arrive at it by I know not how many different practices; they take much trouble to remain in the presence of God in a quantity of ways. Is it not much shorter and more direct to do everything for the love of God, to make use of all the labors of one's state in life to show Him that love, and to maintain His presence within us by this communion of our hearts with His? There is no finesse about it; one has only to do it generously and simply.[2]

Instead of waiting for a warm emotion to respond to, sing a song of praise to Him anyway. Pour out your heart to Him anyway. Thank Him anyway! Honor Him without holding back. Faith does not have to wait for a sign to prove that loving Him will be beneficial this week. Don't hold your affections hostage for the right vibes to come your way first. This is the pathway to richly experiencing a friendship with Jesus.

ACKNOWLEDGE
JESUS

POUR OUT
YOUR HEART

MEDITATE

DEUTERONOMY 6:1-9

REFLECT

Deuteronomy was Moses's last address to Israel before he passed away. He was not addressing the same generation that left Egypt but rather the younger generation that was raised in the wilderness. Having been nomads in the wilderness all their lives, he sought to equip them for the transition of going from wanderers to stewards. They were about to claim the blessing their parents' generation spoke about, and they needed to be spiritually equipped. Verses 4–9 are known in Jewish tradition as the "Shema," which means to "hear" in Hebrew. It became a prayer that was regularly repeated for centuries. It begins with a call for Israel to pay attention, for this was a calling and directive for how Israel was to appropriately respond to God's unfailing love.[3] Before becoming conquerors and before claiming even an inch of land, Moses implored Israel to be lovers of God first. To love God "with all your heart, with all your soul, and with all your strength" was a command (Deuteronomy 6:5). The choice to obey it was meant to be made by faith, not by feeling. Loving God was experienced by obeying His words, meditating on His truth, teaching His words to children, incorporating Him into daily conversations, and even having physical symbols and signs as visual reminders of His nearness. In what ways can you see yourself loving on Jesus this week? What are some practical ways you can create a Presence-centered lifestyle like the one that is described in today's passage?

WEEK ✤ 21

HOST HIS PRESENCE

Once a college student slept in our family's garage. Now, let me explain. I had just given birth to my fourth child, so I was in the daze that postpartum mothers typically go through. My husband was pastoring a young adult ministry at our church, and one of the college students asked him for an emergency favor to temporarily stay in our home before he officially moved into his apartment. Naturally, my husband, being a generous man, welcomed him into our house, thinking he was staying for the weekend. One unforeseen incident led to another, and this student ended up staying for a month! Yet, because no one (not even him) thought he would stay with us for that long, we never made the preparations for him in our home. There was no space for a nineteen-year-old college student in a house filled with four children ages six and under. We never made accommodations for him because we always thought that every weekend or weeknight was his last. Eventually, the dog relieved itself on his pillow, so without us knowing, he quietly and apologetically ended up sleeping in our garage for the rest of his time with us (it was comfy and warm, I promise!). We all laugh about this strange limbo season to this day. We do not have many memories of him being in our house because we never intentionally hosted him. It was as if he was never there!

Sometimes we forget to intentionally host the Holy Spirit as well. We may know that He is with us, but we may not give Him space and welcome Him. Yet, when we do, we give Him permission to influence us and shift our atmosphere. Second Corinthians 3:17 says, "Now the Lord is the Spirit, and where the Spirit of the Lord is, there is freedom." When you make room for Him, you invite the Breaker of Chains to crush your bondage. When you grow in awareness of Him, you sit with the Healer of your broken heart. In your state of confusion, you rest with the Prince of Peace. When you host the Presence of God, you welcome heaven to invade your life.

ACKNOWLEDGE
JESUS

_____

_____

_____

_____

_____

_____

_____

_____

_____

POUR OUT
YOUR HEART

_____

_____

_____

_____

_____

_____

_____

_____

_____

MEDITATE
2 SAMUEL 6:11-15

REFLECT

As the newly appointed king of Israel, David was intent on bringing the ark of the covenant to Jerusalem, the place where the
capital was established. The ark of the covenant was where God's
Presence dwelt, and David knew that the nation of Israel could
not be blessed without Him. Ultimately, David wanted to build
a kingdom centered around the Presence of God. The first attempt to move the ark of the covenant utterly failed (with the
death of Uzzah as a consequence) because they did not inquire
of the Lord about the proper procedures (1 Chronicles 15:13). The
Lord's burning anger caused David to be so discouraged that he
left the ark at Obed-edom's home for three months. When David
heard that there was a visible manifestation of God's favor in
Obed-edom's household, he knew that it was time to try again.
There was exuberant praise and worship along the way, even before the ark was officially relocated to Jerusalem. David leapt and
danced, not as a king but as a child of God. Every step that the
ark was moved in peace was a sign that the Lord had accepted
them and was willing to dwell with them, and that was worthy of
the utmost celebration. Obed-edom housed the Presence of God
as a temporary arrangement. You house the Presence of God in
an eternal covenant. What a wonder! In what ways can you more
intentionally host Him this week?

WEEK  22

GIVE GOD A CHANCE

Do you ever get underwhelmed by your spiritual walk with Jesus? I once read the book of Acts and asked God why my days did not reflect the same experiences. Where were the miracles, signs, and wonders in my life? If God is capable of so much movement, then why did my days look so stagnant? The Holy Spirit was tangible in the book of Acts. The journey the apostles had with Him was so rich, filled with activity worth retelling for centuries to come! I wanted that. I wanted to have my own personal stories with God the way the Christians in the first church did. In my spiritual frustration, I inquired of the Lord, and He inquired back, "Where is your faith?"

You need faith to believe in Jesus, and from the moment you believe in Him, you become a bearer of the Holy Spirit. But you need to activate this faith to become *a partner* of the Holy Spirit for His redemptive activity on earth. Intentional faith-filled actions open the door for the Holy Spirit to move. Taking a chance on God, loving radically, and obeying wholeheartedly give space for God to respond. If you survey the entirety of your life and find that you can live it without the power of the Holy Spirit, then there is a high chance that you have not been activating your faith as of late. You have not witnessed Him do what only He can do because you were busy doing the things you can do on your own.

ACKNOWLEDGE
JESUS

POUR OUT
YOUR HEART

MEDITATE
EZRA 6:16-22

REFLECT

Today's passage is about a celebration, but just a couple of chapters before, the Israelites were stuck. They were returning from exile and were on mission to rebuild the temple of God. However, opposition got in the way and halted their restoration process. Enemies surrounded them and intimidated them, seeking to stop the rebuild. It was not until the prophets Haggai and Zechariah started stirring up the people's faith that the builders chose to take the risk and continue rebuilding the wall. Prophets were God's messengers, servants who listened to Him and delivered His words to the people. God's words have the power to activate our faith, which always leads to action. Consequently, the celebration in today's passage occurred because the Israelites chose to take a chance on their God and recommence the rebuilding of the temple. They took the risk and witnessed God move on their behalf. He delivered them from their opposition through the decree of King Darius. God allowed the restoration to finish in peace. It was the movement of God that made them joyful. If you want to enjoy the victories of God, then you must activate your faith. Sometimes that looks like taking a risk. Other times, it looks like continuing to be faithful and excellent with what is before you. What does activated faith look like for your life this week?

PRAY

WEEK  23

COME OUT OF HIDING

Hiding from God is an instinct as old as time. The moment Adam and Eve realized their disobedience, they conjured up a covering for themselves and hid from their Father (Genesis 3:7–8). When we aren't willing to trust God for mercy and forgiveness, hiding from Him feels safer. When we deal with habits that we don't have the capacity to change, hiding from Jesus is easier. When we don't know what it is like to be treated with compassion and mercy, hiding from God feels natural. No matter how long you have known Him, you can still be holding back your whole self from Jesus. There may be matters that you refuse to address with Him because you fear how He will respond. You may not even want to deal with these dark places, let alone have God deal with them. Shame makes us feel like we are safer alone than in God's hands.

Friend of God, let's come out of hiding this week. If we want to enrich our intimacy with His Presence, then we must confess to Him more honestly. Let's go beyond the niceties and the facade of do-gooderies. There is a TikTok account that leaves a microphone on and allows people, with their backs turned to the camera, to openly confess their most confidential matters. Everything from secret hatreds, childhood trauma, and unconfessed crime has been revealed. A sobering reality is that everyone knew this was only possible because it was anonymous, and most people feel safer holding on to their shameful burdens alone. But God is not like any human on earth, and *He does not respond as we do.* When you honestly confess the ugliness of your motives, He meets you with compassion and forgiveness. When you vulnerably reveal even your irreverent doubts toward Him, He meets you with grace and strength. The Presence of God is our refuge—a safe place. Our truth can be entrusted to Him. He will handle it with care. Draw close, friend of God.

ACKNOWLEDGE
JESUS

POUR OUT
YOUR HEART

MEDITATE
PSALM 32

REFLECT

We miss out on great joy when we avoid God! David instructs us not to avoid God because of transgressions, sins, and iniquity. He illustrates his experience of what it was like to hide from God; it began with, "When I kept silent" (verse 3). What does hiding from God look like for you, friend? Could it be avoiding confession of your wrongdoings? Could it be halfheartedly worshiping due to jadedness? Could it be avoiding church because you do not want to deal with your shame? He warns us not to be like a horse or mule "that must be controlled with bit and bridle or else it will not come near you" (verse 9). Have you noticed all the ways He acts on behalf of those who acknowledge Him while being honest with themselves? He protects them (verse 7). He delivers them (verse 7). He will surround them with faithful love (verse 10). God intends to do so much good for those who draw near, but He will not force anyone to return to Him. He will not threaten you. It is far better to return to Him in your mess than to remain silent and apart from God. There is no requirement to fix yourself before you return. Approach Him as you are, and allow yourself to feel the pang of confession for a moment so that your soul can be refreshed with His gracious love for a lifetime. Is there any way that you have been hiding from the Presence of God? Can you ask the Holy Spirit to reveal what you should bring to Him in confession today?

PRAY

WEEK ✿ 24

DEAD ENDS

"I can't" is one of the most liberating confessions we can make before God, but it is a vulnerable process to get to this place. Because it can feel like defeat, we usually fight to ensure that we never get to such a humbling spot. Self-reliance seems so much safer. Being truly dependent on God can feel uneasy. Our busyness seems more reliable than waiting for His deliverance and help. Although attempting to be the master of our own lives leads to stress and angst, we often still prefer the self-sufficient path. We are willing to clench our jaws, recalculate the plan, and consider too many other people's opinions because we trust ourselves more than we trust Jesus.

We do all this to maintain a semblance of control, anything to avoid that scary place of . . .

- powerlessness
- helplessness
- hopelessness
- loneliness

We would rather create another plan, keep ourselves busy, or harden our hearts to avoid the dreaded dead end—where every dream has been spent and no ideas are left, where you are counting change and have nowhere else to turn. It may be a dead end to your ways, but it is the beginning of God's way. Do not despair, for a kind and gentle Friend awaits you there. He woos you to depend on His voice rather than strive by your own willpower. He encourages you to know the Architect rather than try to configure the blueprint on your own. He welcomes you in this moment to know Him more intimately than you know your troubles, for even in your anguish, you can still enjoy friendship with Him. Because when you can't . . . He will.

ACKNOWLEDGE
JESUS

_____
_____
_____
_____
_____
_____
_____
_____
_____
_____

POUR OUT
YOUR HEART

_____
_____
_____
_____
_____
_____
_____
_____
_____
_____

MEDITATE

ZECHARIAH 4:6-10

REFLECT

As referenced before in Week 22, Zechariah and Haggai were
God's messengers to the Jewish people in a time when recon-
struction efforts for the temple were stalled from harsh opposition (Ezra 5). The passage we just read was one of Zechariah's
prophesies that lit up the faith of the people once paralyzed in
fear. The word Zechariah received here was also specifically for
Zerubbabel, a man who had the position to govern the Israelites
but had very little power to lead them. Zechariah's prophecy in-
cluded this divine encouragement: "Not by strength or by might,
but by my Spirit" (verse 6). It was God's call for His people to allow great effort to make way for great faith instead. They were
in a situation where their best intentions to do what was right
did not measure up. It was not enough back then, just as our
best efforts aren't always enough today. It had to be by His Spirit.
Although the Israelites were at this discouraging impasse, they
needed to be in this dilemma to admit their dependence on God's
grace and fully pass the responsibility of their fate to His hands.
By His Spirit, we are endowed with another level of empower-
ment, where we will be able to face our greatest obstacles and
boldly declare, "What are *you*, great mountain?" Friend of God,
are you still depending on your strength and might? What are the
mountains that you face this week?

WEEK  25

ASK FOR HELP

Friend of God, what are your needs this week? If you're like me, I am sure you have several. Although doing a devotional, such as this one, meets our spiritual needs, God does care for our physical and emotional needs as well. If Jesus were only interested in our spiritual needs, then He would not have fed the five thousand (Matthew 14:13–21). He would not have healed the sick. He would not have looked upon the widow weeping for her dead son with such compassion and stopped in His tracks to raise him to life (Luke 7:11–17). Not only do your needs matter to God, but He wants to help. Jesus lived a fully human life, so He understands physical limitations and emotional hurt. In the Gospels, Jesus took the needs of humankind as opportunities to draw closer to them. The God we pray to is not aloof to our daily concerns.

Friend of God, the Holy Spirit is a Helper. Having someone who is reliable, powerful, and available to you is an absolute gift. Let's be real: It's hard to ask just anyone for help. Even among your friends, you wouldn't approach just anyone with your needs. You would have to be in good standing and have confidence in the one you approach. Sometimes, you may wait to earn enough favor from someone before you ask anything of them. It's vulnerable, too, because when you ask someone who has the power to help you, you also give them the power to reject you. Not only does God invite you to approach Him, but *He invites you to approach Him boldly,* for it says in Hebrews 4:16, "Let us approach the throne of grace with boldness, so that we may receive mercy and find grace to help us in time of need." So, let's not wait until after we grumble about it for days or until we get to the point of utter desperation. Let's boldly approach Him and enjoy our friendship with the Helper.

ACKNOWLEDGE
JESUS

_____
_____
_____
_____
_____
_____
_____
_____
_____
_____

POUR OUT
YOUR HEART

_____
_____
_____
_____
_____
_____
_____
_____
_____
_____

MEDITATE

JOHN 16:19-24

REFLECT

Here Jesus describes what will happen at His crucifixion and resurrection. He promises the disciples that enduring the painful
mystery of His crucifixion would be worth it because it would pave
the way for their own access to the Father. Up until this point, the
disciples followed Jesus and witnessed Him walk in sonship with
His Heavenly Father. Jesus lived His life on earth with access to
the resources of heaven because He approached the Father for
His every necessity. Although Jesus is fully God, He was fully man
in this world. Therefore, the provision and power Jesus lived by
were the fruit of His access to the Father. After the resurrection,
the disciples, too, had the same access to the Father that Jesus
did during His ministry on earth. You do too. Not only do Christians have this access, but we are also encouraged to utilize it so
that we can experience great joy. Have you been accessing your
Father lately? One way to enjoy friendship with God is by asking
Him for help through prayer and then being open to receiving His
blessing. Jesus calls us to do this "so that your joy may be complete" (verse 24). The pleasure here is not merely in the answered
prayers, but in the fact that we as mere humans can directly approach our King and call Him Father. If you had no doubt that your
Father in heaven would care about your needs and respond to
your prayers, what would you ask of Him this week?

WEEK  26

WHAT GIVES YOU POWER?

Humans have an affinity for power. They either want it for themselves, or they want to be around it. Now, before you dismiss this as irrelevant to you, remember that power comes in different forms! For some, people's opinions of us are our power. For others, it could be what is in our bank accounts. Reputation, appearance, status at work . . . you name it. We care about these things because they elevate and enable us. Without them, we feel vulnerable, incapable, and perhaps even unworthy. Friend of God, what tends to give you power these days? You will recognize it by how you feel when it is threatened. For me, my power used to be from what I was able to accomplish. I didn't realize that until I became a mom of four little children within five and a half years. I was thrust into a season where my life goals had to be placed on the back burner, and for a while, I didn't feel like myself. I questioned who I was and what I was living for (lack of sleep would do that to you too). Although I felt powerless, I thank God for that season because otherwise I would have never recognized what I depended on.

Our power as friends of God is not in what we have or do, but rather in *who we are submitted to*. We do not need to be better, know more, accrue accolades, or achieve greatness. Friend of God, you can be at your absolute worst today. You may be drained of physical or emotional energy. You may feel that you do not have a true friend or anything to be genuinely proud of. Yet here's the kicker—you can be your weakest self and still be a powerful friend of God. What joy! So, ask Him to be with you in your brokenness. Yield yourself completely to Him and know this: You can still do the things that only God can do simply because He is with you.

ACKNOWLEDGE
JESUS

_____
_____
_____
_____
_____
_____
_____
_____
_____
_____

POUR OUT
YOUR HEART

_____
_____
_____
_____
_____
_____
_____
_____
_____
_____

MEDITATE
ACTS 3:1-10

REFLECT

This story started with the despair of a crippled man and ended with leaps of praise. And yet, the conduits for this moment were not rich men with lots of influence. They did not even have what the man was begging for. Sometimes, because we assume that we do not know much or have much, we may overlook the opportunities around us to show up with the Holy Spirit's power. The reality is the disciples did not have resources to spare. In the worldly sense, they did not have any power at all, and they sure did not hide it! In fact, they openly confessed what they did not have. Peter and John were not afraid to appear weak because, although they had nothing, they were rich in the Presence of God. So, if they didn't have silver or gold, what *did* they have? They had authority from their Good Friend Jesus to bring good news in a bad moment. They carried the power to heal and evangelize because of their friendship with God. Your lack today is no obstacle to your ability to experience God's redemptive power at work. You, too, may not have silver or gold. You may not even have the motivation to get out of bed. You may not have influence over the masses or talent to move a crowd. But you can give what you have, which is Jesus Christ of Nazareth.

WEEK  27

GOD IS A GIVER

Life can be demanding. Even as I write these very words, I have notifications ringing on my phone, the washer in the laundry room alerting me to switch out my load, and a list reminding me of how I'm behind on pretty much everything. There are expectations everywhere. Whether you are a young student feeling hounded by new math concepts or an elderly man attempting to navigate the pressures of a new season, life doesn't stop. Not only this, but people can ask much of you. It could be that one person who requires an extra dose of attentiveness, that text that needs to be answered, or that partner who needs more time. When we are overwhelmed, it's because we find ourselves sinking in a sea of endless demands whirling around us.

Life may be demanding, but God is a *giver*, which is why friendship with Him is so sweet. He loved us so much that He *gave* His Son (John 3:16). Jesus did not come to be served but to serve (Mark 10:45). Yes, living for Him requires much, but it doesn't leave us empty. He does not demand from us just to be satiated or appeased. On the contrary, *He asks of us so that He can give to us.* Therefore, as we commit to doing all things for Him and with Him, our friendship with Jesus becomes a heavenly oasis amid life's daily pressures.

ACKNOWLEDGE
JESUS

_____
_____
_____
_____
_____
_____
_____
_____
_____
_____

POUR OUT
YOUR HEART

_____
_____
_____
_____
_____
_____
_____
_____
_____
_____

122

MEDITATE

ACTS 13:42-52

REFLECT

A lot of things were not going Paul and Barnabas's way in today's passage, causing friction. Here they were, being faithful to what God had called them to do and ministering in Antioch. And although many seemed to be receptive to the gospel at first, the Jewish people began to stir up persecution against them. How terribly disappointing! However, despite the rejection, the insults, and the growing opposition, the gospel still spread and Paul and Barnabas were protected. Actually, they were more than protected. Verse 52 recounts how Paul and Barnabas were "filled with joy and the Holy Spirit." Now, let's be frank. When things do not go as I had hoped, I am patient at best. Filled with joy? Not likely. Although their agenda was being challenged and their work was misunderstood by many, they were so complete in the Presence of God that they could shake off the negativity and move on. Paul and Barnabas found this vitality in the Spirit as they dedicated their lives to following Him, even when it was toward pain. While Paul and Barnabas gave it their all to spread the gospel, the Holy Spirit ensured that they were not left void of fulfillment and strength. Despite the bumps along the road, they thrived because they were in friendship with Him. Friend of God, in what ways can you intentionally do all things for Jesus and with Jesus this week?

PRAY

WEEK  28

WHEN STUCK

Have you ever been stuck in prayer? Even if you're in the right space at the right time with the right music on, you might still find yourself sitting before Jesus with nothing to say. It seems like any words you muster just fall back to the ground . . . ignored and unheard by God. In these moments, when the atmosphere around us feels dead and abandoned, our souls search for reasons why we aren't sensing a response from Him. Some of those reasons can lead you to condemn yourself. You may be on the floor in your bedroom blaming yourself for not being disciplined enough to reach Him or spiritual enough to hear Him. Alternatively, you could end up blaming God for abandoning you or being unwilling to help you. Ultimately, when the stillness during your prayers discourages you, it's because you are misinterpreting the quiet as an indictment against God's goodness or your worthiness.

Friend of God, it is not your responsibility to extinguish silence between you and the Holy Spirit. If you have no words to say, then you can just sit with the awareness that He is with you—He really is with you. Just as the silence between companions can be meaningful, so can this stillness between you and the Holy Spirit. You may feel stuck, but that does not stop God from moving in your life.

Here is a truth you can hold to this week, one that will keep you praying: God adores you, and He is sitting with you right now. Take a deep breath and let go of any assumptions you have about the "right" way to experience Him. When you draw closer to Him, He draws closer to you, whether you sense it or not (James 4:8). Be gentle with yourself because even Christ does not condemn you. Keep listening for Him and talking to Him—not as a beggar or a dejected stranger but as a friend.

ACKNOWLEDGE
JESUS

POUR OUT
YOUR HEART

MEDITATE

ROMANS 8:18-30

REFLECT

Let's start with some context today. In Romans 8, the apostle Paul exhorts the believers to live by the Holy Spirit. A fun fact to note is that the Holy Spirit is mentioned nineteen times in this chapter alone! It is the believer's manifesto, a proclamation of freedom. This is for all believers. This is for you. Throughout Romans 8, Paul explains the many layers of freedom we are called to enjoy in the Spirit, such as freedom from condemnation and freedom from ties to our old self. Today's verses establish the unbreakable insurance we have as believers. *God is with us and for us.* This is your security, blood-bought by Christ. This is His promise, sealed by the Holy Spirit. If you have no words to say, He will intercede on your behalf. Even if you fail, He will work all things together for your good. Even if you feel as though you are going backward in life, His hands will lovingly work through your mess until it is glorious. This is the ultimate level of freedom. You are never without the Helper, the Redeemer, the Teacher, the Counselor, the Comforter, and so on! So, even if it feels like your worship songs are reaching no one and your prayers are being met with silence, you can still confidently smile and assuredly know that your Good Friend is right there with you. The cross assures us of this. How can this truth help you enjoy prayer this week?

WEEK  29

ENJOYING THE CREATOR

Peace, love, and joy are some of the most expensive and sought-after commodities on this earth. Pause for a moment to consider this with me. Imagine how much goes into the security systems and insurance plans for our "just in case" situations. We will pay a high price for peace of mind. How much effort do we expend enhancing ourselves to attract people to us? Or perhaps even to keep people with us? We will do what it takes for love, or at least our limited version of love. Let us consider how patterns like substance abuse, addiction, and screen time are sometimes an escape from pain and a mirage of momentary happiness. When we are hungry for joy, we will use any measure to fill that void—even at the cost of our well-being.

Humankind is endlessly chasing after things that we were never meant to *find on our own; only God* can give us peace, love, and joy. The Creator is the originator of these qualities and all that is good. The world can only imitate God's blessings, yet we are quick to look for means and methods to create these things apart from the Presence of God. In doing so, we constantly fall short. Isn't it tiring? Perhaps the way to attain all that is good is not in trying harder but rather in resting with Jesus. Sync your heart with His. Mold your thoughts after His thoughts. Acknowledge His Presence and appreciate His nearness. He can create whatever good you do not have within you at this time.

ACKNOWLEDGE
JESUS

POUR OUT
YOUR HEART

MEDITATE

GALATIANS 5:19-25

REFLECT

Although your flesh is prone to produce sin, you are not obligated to practice it. Our carnality is drawn to vices such as idolatry and selfish ambition because we expect them to produce the peace, love, and joy we crave. It is difficult to give up pleasures, even in the name of doing what is religiously right, when we suspect that we will be left empty and dissatisfied. However, your proclivity to immorality is not your master and certainly not your friend. Instead of practicing sin, practice the Presence of God instead! The key is in verse 25: the call to keep in step with the Holy Spirit. We keep in step with Him by intentionally being aware of His Presence throughout the day and following His ways. Intentionally cultivate intimacy with Jesus and obey His words. Do things as Jesus would. Think about His truth from Scripture. Abide by His directions. Ask Him for His opinions. Consider His feelings. The apostle Paul calls us to bear the Spirit's fruit, not conjure up our own fruit. It was never about trying to make ourselves happier and better by our own means. What an exhausting endeavor! We are simply to follow Him, step-by-step. As we prioritize His ways over ours, transformation begins.

PRAY

WEEK  30

SHIFT YOUR FOCUS

There was once a time, on December 31, when I was going to write a journal entry to reflect on the previous year. Holding my pen, I was ready to go on and on about how it was the roughest of years, yet I seemed to have made it through. I had all the melancholy words on hand to lament over how hard it had been. But before I began, I started to go through the photo album on my phone to recall all the events that transpired that year. I had thousands of photographs and videos, and by the end of it, I had a change of heart. My inner being was practically leaping with thanksgiving. You see, I had forgotten what God had done. I was not aware of just how many breakthroughs, victories, and gains there were that year. For months, I had mistakenly felt that I was waiting for God to bless me. Yet when I directly brought to my awareness what He had done, my feelings changed. Friend of God, what you are aware of will determine what you experience.

As you prepare yourself to enjoy the Presence of God, what are you most aware of right now? Your attention may be focused on something else, perhaps even someone else. You may read these words with the best of intentions but struggle to shift your focus away from the clutter on your table. Faith in this moment can look like an offering of your attention to Jesus. It is as simple as that. You may feel pressured to have things to say or to address problems with Him right away. However, sometimes all you need to do is adore Him and appreciate what He's done. We magnify what we focus on. With your whole being, place a spotlight on the Holy Spirit and dwell there. Our awareness of His Presence will grow when we set our internal gaze on Him.

ACKNOWLEDGE
JESUS

_____
_____
_____
_____
_____
_____
_____
_____
_____
_____
_____

POUR OUT
YOUR HEART

_____
_____
_____
_____
_____
_____
_____
_____
_____
_____
_____

MEDITATE
PHILIPPIANS 4:2-9

REFLECT

The apostle Paul acknowledges that there are disagreements and conflicts among the Philippians, notably between Euodia and Syntyche. Yet he urges them to be aware of God's Presence despite their issues. He reminds them to rejoice in Him. He says it twice, even! Why? Because the Lord is near. Although their reasons for being anxious are real, Paul encourages the Philippians to take their attention away from their fears by choosing to not worry about anything. We can be so accommodating to our apprehensions and nagging concerns, but the instruction here is clear. Do not worry about anything. Instead, raise your awareness of God's Presence by giving thanks and bringing every concern to Him in prayer. Paul calls the Philippians to interrupt their natural way of negative thinking and shift their focus to God while dwelling in the reality of His goodness. The apostle Paul is not commanding the Philippians to ignore their problems, for you can still be aware of your problems while choosing to gaze into the good He has already done. Enjoying God's Presence is possible even when there are problems to fix and pain to deal with. You do it by giving Him your attention and enriching your awareness of His nearness.

WEEK ❁ 31

OUR JOYFUL KING

I remember feeling nervous when it came time to meet my husband's (at that time my fiancé's) grandmother. In Korean and Korean American culture, the elderly in families are highly esteemed. Their opinions are held in high regard, and their approval matters deeply. To meet the matriarch of my husband's large family was not something I took lightly. As I entered her home, I felt like I was stepping on holy ground. You see, she wasn't just any Korean American grandmother. She was a devout Christian, one of the first to believe in her family line. So, it wasn't just cultural expectations that I had to meet but religious standards as well. The walls had portraits of Korean Bible verses, and her own large print Bible was laid open on the dining table. She sauntered over from the kitchen, apron-clad and with arms wide open. I wasn't sure what I was anticipating, but it sure wasn't the warm embrace that I received. She rubbed my back and smiled, telling me in Korean that she had been waiting for me. I was taken aback by such a joyful welcome. I approached her home fully expecting to earn her favor, but instead I was surprised by her delight.

Friend of God, did you know that Jesus is joyful? Yes, the Bible is clear that the Holy Spirit can be both grieved and quenched. Furthermore, during His time on earth, Jesus felt a wide range of emotions, and many of them were negative. Yet He was also full of joy (Hebrews 12:2). And even now on this day, He is full of joy. God takes pleasure in communing with you. Although the cross was excruciating, He was glad to pay the price—for you. His countenance is not a scowl. His voice is not impatient and cold. Even as you are about to approach Him, He is ready to receive you with kindness and mercy!

ACKNOWLEDGE
JESUS

_____
_____
_____
_____
_____
_____
_____
_____
_____
_____

POUR OUT
YOUR HEART

_____
_____
_____
_____
_____
_____
_____
_____
_____

MEDITATE
HEBREWS 1:5-9

REFLECT

The author of Hebrews begins his letter by extolling Jesus above all creatures and things. In the days of the first churches, people received the news of Jesus with a wide range of responses. Some saw Him as a prophet but not Messiah. There was also a misconception that Jesus was no higher than the angels. In response to all this, the Hebrew author aimed to set the record straight. Not only is Jesus superior to all beings, but He is ruler of all. Despite being among us flawed and broken people, He is anointed with the "oil of joy" (verse 9). This oil is literally translated from Greek as "olive oil," which often symbolizes the presence and power of the Holy Spirit. Even during His ministry on earth, which led Him to an execution on the cross, Jesus was empowered with joy. Despite being a ruler of the fallen and the feeble, He is our happy King! He is glad to save you. This is reminiscent of what is later said of Him in Hebrews 12:2, "For the joy that lay before him, he endured the cross." How might this alter the way you experience Him this week? How do you feel about communing with your happy King today?

WEEK ✤ 32

DAY BY DAY

Hey, friend of God, I'd love to be a bit more vulnerable with you today. As a preacher of the gospel, I get to share a lot of stories about my mountaintop moments with God—the highlight reels of how He showed up for me throughout my faith journey. I have a dramatic turnaround story: I was a sixteen-year-old girl struggling with depression when I encountered God at a youth camp in Mexico. The instant I experienced the touch of the Holy Spirit, my appetite for this world was completely ruined. The thing is, as fantastic as my salvation story is, I struggled to consistently enjoy my relationship with Jesus for at least the first decade of my Christian walk. Although I loved His Presence, I did not live a Presence-centered life. I lived a self-centered life, and I just wanted God to endorse it. The biblical standards to live by felt overbearing with impossible rules. The traditions did not appeal to me right away. Engaging with a Christian community was intimidating and at times even hurtful. I loved Jesus but hated religious pressure (either self-imposed or from church culture), and I didn't know how to navigate that tension for quite some time.

But one day, my friend looked at me quizzically and said, "You've changed." She was a childhood friend I spent every summer with. The first day together when we reunited for another summer, she thoughtfully listened to me and watched me, only to later make that comment. I had changed. What she meant was that I was happier. Calmer. More easygoing. She sensed a peace in me and wanted to know where it came from. What had happened was that I spent the whole year prior beginning to release my desires to God. I was tired of grappling with my Maker. Having one foot on the boat of obedience and the other foot on the dock of disobedience kept my faith paralyzed. Truth be told, it was not an overnight transformation. Rather, it was a daily surrender. I had to say yes to Jesus again and again. And even though I did not always feel it, change was happening inside me.

ACKNOWLEDGE
JESUS

_____
_____
_____
_____
_____
_____
_____
_____
_____
_____

POUR OUT
YOUR HEART

_____
_____
_____
_____
_____
_____
_____
_____
_____
_____

MEDITATE

JUDE 17-25

REFLECT

Jude warned the early Christians of false teachers and heretics who could cause them to stray from their faith in Christ. These people lived according to their own ungodly desires instead of following the guidance of the Holy Spirit. Acting as masters of their own lives, they did whatever they wanted. In our culture, discontented grumbling, living for oneself, arrogant words, and flattering people for personal gain are not considered to be the worst of vices. Selfishness can masquerade as wisdom, especially today. Jude warns us of this. You may not be a heretic, but you may be tempted to live a self-centered life. The culture we live in pressures us to submit to the vortex of constant want, but Jude encourages us to invest in our faith and continuously commune with the Holy Spirit instead. The best way to engage in the spiritual warfare of our time is by building a Presence-centered life that is dedicated to knowing and following God. We accomplish this with simple acts of devotion each day: nurturing our faith, praying, growing in love with God, and anticipating Christ's eventual return. When Jesus returns, you and I will be ecstatic with joy, and every little and big yes we gave Him throughout our days will have been worth it. What does a Presence-centered life look like for you? What little shifts can you make in your daily routine and perspective to live for Jesus?

ENJOYING HIS FRIENDSHIP IN PRISONS, STORMS, *and* EVERYTHING MUNDANE

WEEK 🌿 33

HE IS WITH YOU

Have you ever stopped going to Jesus because your circumstances felt void of His Presence? Every night, when I was six years old, I sought the Lord. I had an innate longing to connect with the Creator of the universe. With the lights off and my bedroom door closed, I placed the blanket over my head and talked to God in my mind. Having never been to church, I did not know how else to pray. I asked Him to speak to me, but I heard only silence. I asked Him to reveal Himself to me, but all I saw was the darkness. One day I watched a gospel film on a family vacation and learned that God's name was Jesus, so I sought Him. But I still didn't experience anything that satiated my seeking. By middle school, I became jaded and I wanted nothing to do with God. During that time, my mother became the first believer in our family, and she said the only prayers. She became great friends with the Holy Spirit. One rainy evening on our way home from violin lessons, she said, "I talked to God about you yesterday." Like a typical preteen child, I nonchalantly responded, "Okay. What did He say?" To which my mother replied, "God said He remembers how you sought Him with all your heart as a child." The car was silent for the rest of the ride.

I ran to my room as soon as the car pulled into the garage. I buried my face in my pillow and wept. "You know me," I whispered. Up until that point, I believed that my prayers went nowhere. But He had been there the entire time—listening, watching, and remembering. Although I did not dedicate my life to Christ until two years later, this revelation changed my trajectory toward Him.

Friend of God, I cannot pretend to know what you are enduring in this hour. Even so, I do know that pain can consume our senses and leave us feeling like He isn't there. But keep whispering your requests. Allow sorrow to surface and well up into tears, for tears can pray too. He is with you.

ACKNOWLEDGE
JESUS

_____
_____
_____
_____
_____
_____
_____
_____
_____
_____

POUR OUT
YOUR HEART

_____
_____
_____
_____
_____
_____
_____
_____
_____
_____

MEDITATE

GENESIS 28:10-19

REFLECT

Jacob left his home and all he had known to run from his brother Esau's wrath. Not only did he face the heartbreak of leaving his family home and the fear of being killed by his vengeful brother, but there was also the fear of the unknown. Would he be okay? Was there a future for him? Yet the moment he rested, the Lord revealed to him in a dream that His Presence was with him. God said, "*Look*, I am with you and will watch over you wherever you go" (verse 15, emphasis added). Amid the chaos and discouragement, Jacob was not aware of the goodness of God so close beside him. Yet once he realized that the Presence of God was in his midst, he proclaimed, "What an awesome place this is!" (verse 17). Just the night before, this was forlorn ground, a temporary resting place he found after being stripped of everything he held dear. Now, it was an awesome place because he was aware of God's Presence. Friend of God, the glory of His Presence does not just reside at Bethel; it resides in us as well, thanks to the blood of Christ. We do not need to wait for a dream to confirm this because we have the guarantee of the cross. What are some ways you can meditate on this truth today?

WEEK ✿ 34

THE EXTRAORDINARY IN THE ORDINARY

Have you ever read through the Old and New Testaments and felt like an outsider looking into someone else's grand experience with God? When we consider how Samuel heard His voice as a child, how Elijah called forth fire from the heavens, and how Isaiah saw the splendor of the King, our casual trip to the grocery store can feel irrelevant to redemptive history. Most of our days do not look like the eventful testimonies that show up on a church stage or get recorded for social media. In reality, they likely look ordinary, regular, and mundane. When we are responding to emails and vacuuming the corners of the room, is God's glory still with us? It may not seem like it when we mistakenly equate the uneventful day-to-day with living a faithless life.

Friend of God, what makes a life supernatural is not the absence of the natural. Rather, it is in the inclusion of the Holy Spirit. Some forget that Mary, one of the most iconic figures in the Bible, spent most of her days doing what mothers do. She made food, washed clothes, and was faithful with what was before her. What made her life supernatural was that she said yes to the Holy Spirit. To this day, she has accomplished nothing that is lauded in the worldly sense. She just remained with Him, and in doing so, she didn't miss out on what God was doing. The daily ordinary is not proof of your kingdom insignificance. God's power is in your obedience, not in great feats and hype. So, pour that second cup of coffee. Take that long commute. Change the oil in your car, and go to that doctor's appointment. And do it with joy because you do not have to chase the extraordinary to build a real and vibrant life with Jesus.

ACKNOWLEDGE
JESUS

_____
_____
_____
_____
_____
_____
_____
_____
_____
_____

POUR OUT
YOUR HEART

_____
_____
_____
_____
_____
_____
_____
_____
_____
_____

MEDITATE
EXODUS 3:1-6

REFLECT

At this point in Moses's story, he had fled from his life in the palace of Egypt and was living in Midian. He married a Midianite woman named Zipporah and spent forty years in voluntary exile (Acts 7:30). For forty years, he lived as a husband, father, and steward of his responsibilities. No one treated him like royalty or the chosen leader of Israel. In fact, he ran into the burning bush as he was shepherding his father-in-law's flock. He wasn't looking for a burning bush, and he wasn't looking for an experience to upgrade his status. Moses's friendship with God was built as he stewarded his daily responsibilities and followed God's lead. Amid the mundane, God spoke to Moses, but not in a way that he expected. In verse 3, we see that Moses thought, "I must go over and look at this remarkable sight." Two things happened here. Moses paused what he was doing. Then he went out of his way to investigate. He must have seen it from far away to want to go take a closer look. This was something that he could have walked past and ignored. If God were to interrupt you today, would you be willing to pay attention? Would you ever pause in response to an unction of the Holy Spirit? We can still be excellent stewards of our day-to-day while being alert and open to what God wants to do through us and for us.

PRAY

WEEK  35

BELIEVE GOD, NOT FEAR

Fear grows when we search for security in anything or anyone other than God. I'm typically never afraid of heights, but I do recall the occasion when my family and I were driving over a tall bridge. It was fiercely windy that day, and I felt a slight sway. I was not sure whether it was the car or the bridge itself, but it was enough to make my entire body tense up. I was paralyzed, and worst-case scenarios ran through my mind. I am sure the bridge was dependable, as it had been for years. After all, it is not every day that you see cars flying off bridges. But even if we place our security in the 99.99 percent guarantee, that .01 percent can still be reason enough to be afraid. Fear is riled over the shadows of slight foreboding possibilities.

The truth is, placing our security in God does not guarantee that things will go *our* way. The only guarantee is that He is with you and that His way will be for your good (Romans 8:28). Now, if you are anything like me, that statement may not fully satisfy you yet. Many of us have real issues that desperately require help. Fear aggressively demands our attention. Yet, here's the thing—God is not afraid. He is not frantic. He is not pacing to and fro, brooding over our fears. He is not up all night like we are. In Him, it's never a 99.99 percent guarantee that it will work out for our good and His glory. It is 100 percent. Let's fix our eyes on the 100 percent.

ACKNOWLEDGE
JESUS

_____
_____
_____
_____
_____
_____
_____
_____
_____
_____

POUR OUT
YOUR HEART

_____
_____
_____
_____
_____
_____
_____
_____
_____
_____

MEDITATE
JUDGES 6:11-16

REFLECT

Gideon was afraid. When the Lord called him, he was threshing wheat in a hidden place to avoid his enemies. Yet the angel of the Lord appeared to him and said two things: The Presence of God was with him, and he was a valiant warrior. Neither felt true to Gideon. Sometimes we must agree with God's truth before we experience it. When was the last time you asked God for His perspective over your situation? I'm sure you will be surprised at what God sees. Gideon continued to retort with all his "what ifs" and "buts," all to which the Lord just repeated, "I will be with you" (verse 16). He did not respond to Gideon's fears but spoke gently and firmly to his soul instead. God reminded him of His Presence. Although Gideon kept pointing to the dire situation and the re-ality of his own weaknesses, the Lord assured him of only one thing: "I will be with you." Sometimes, we can be like Gideon. Instead of asking God what He sees in us, we may be immersed in our own self-condemnation and shame. Instead of asking God what He will do in our situation, we can be quick to believe in the fracture in our family, our dire financial status, or the rejection letters. Fear follows our physical senses—what we see, hear, and feel. Faith follows the voice of God. How will you make room for God's voice this week? What are the fears that you need to stop following today?

PRAY

WEEK ❧ 36

Friend of God, let's rejoice this week. Yep, you read that right. You may not want to, and you may not even know what that could look like amid your current circumstances. You may also think that rejoicing is only for something you've been waiting for. Your cheer may be waiting on a breakthrough in your health. Your gladness and thanksgiving may be waiting until you accomplish something worthwhile. Your relief and jubilation may be waiting until you've earned the right to rejoice. You may even be waiting to testify about Jesus until He does what you need Him to do. Joy that requires external affirmation is merely fleeting happiness because it is dependent on a fallen world. True joy comes when those who carry the Holy Spirit also believe in what He is doing. We may not understand what He is doing, *but we can believe in it,* nonetheless.

God calls us to rejoice *by faith.* This means appreciating what God is up to before the results are even in. It's being in alignment with heaven regardless of what is happening on earth. It's knowing that bad news is just incomplete news. Faith chooses to trust in His goodness more than in the storm. Faith calls us to believe His faithfulness more than the despair from closed doors. Faith enjoys His unconditional acceptance in the face of rejection. It gives us permission to dance amid broken dreams. Even in the stillness of being alone and confused, you can be sure of this: God is doing something worth being thankful for. As long as you breathe, you can rejoice.

ACKNOWLEDGE
JESUS

_____
_____
_____
_____
_____
_____
_____
_____
_____
_____

POUR OUT
YOUR HEART

_____
_____
_____
_____
_____
_____
_____
_____
_____
_____

MEDITATE
NEHEMIAH 8:8-12

REFLECT

After the Israelites were exiled from their homeland, a remnant of God's people survived. God opened doors, through the leadership of Nehemiah and Ezra, to return the people to Jerusalem and rebuild their walls. The Israelites were aware that the exile occurred because of their own disobedience and folly. So, their return to Jerusalem was not a valiant one. They were disgraced at the state of their city. After the wall had been rebuilt and more exiles returned, the people wanted the book of the law to be read aloud. However, it turned out to be a stark reminder of how far they had fallen. Restoration felt impossible at this point. The remorse was deep. Weeping ensued. Yet, leaders exhorted the people: It was not enough to wail regretfully over what they had done. Instead, they must rejoice over what God had done. Although all they saw around them was evidence of their failure, they were called to be glad by faith! Regret and shame make us feel disqualified from God's blessing. Friend of God, it does little for you to spend your days fixated on where you have gone wrong. Let us thank God for what He has done right for us, and let us do so with all our might. Let us rejoice over a God who forgives and restores. Let us tell people about His unconditional love. Let us hold tight to the words in the Bible that can guide us through trouble.

PRAY

WEEK  37

REVEAL YOURSELF

As a pastor, I frequently witness people sitting in their cars in the church parking lot on Sunday mornings. Although it's not something I look for, I cannot help but catch someone taking a few minutes alone in their car to compose themself before entering the building for the worship service. Sometimes it's to sit in silence before they must show their "Sunday best." Sometimes it's to fix their makeup after the unstoppable tears during the car ride over. On occasion, there is a couple who needs to complete their heated argument before opening the car doors and pretending like all is well. Rarely do we feel comfortable showing people our *real* selves. Small talk and a positive countenance are armor for those who do not feel safe to reveal what is truly going on within.

Friend of God, Jesus is not surprised by what is within you. Lamentations 3:22–23 says, "Because of the LORD's great love we are not consumed, for his compassions never fail. They are new every morning; great is your faithfulness" (NIV). The Holy Spirit is fiercely loyal. Even at your worst, He remains. Even if you are reading these words halfheartedly with barely a desire to call upon Him for help, He dwells with you still. This is not because He is a pushover of any kind; rather, His divine love is not changed by our lack of love. His affection toward us cannot be tainted by our waywardness. He remains perfectly good, even while we are extremely imperfect. Let us interrupt the storm within by greeting the Holy Spirit. Utter the unspeakable, and share what's undisclosed to others. Tell Him everything. Suppress nothing. Grace awaits you.

ACKNOWLEDGE
JESUS

_____
_____
_____
_____
_____
_____
_____
_____
_____
_____

POUR OUT
YOUR HEART

_____
_____
_____
_____
_____
_____
_____
_____
_____
_____

MEDITATE
PSALM 73:21-28

REFLECT

The psalmist envied those who chose to live their lives as strangers to God. He struggled with something modern-day Christians still grapple with—being convinced that it is worth knowing God and being set apart for Him. When remaining faithful to Jesus is costly to you, the carefree apathy of those who do not know Him can look like bliss. The psalmist was bitter about his faith journey and was tempted to believe that it was not worth it. It brought about a foolishness in him that he was not proud of. Even still—God never left him. This realization set in for the psalmist at verse 23. Not only did God remain with him, but He protected him, guided him, and strengthened him even still. All that came out of the psalmist was an unimpressive admission of his weakness, but with this, he acknowledged God. He chose to struggle in His Presence (as opposed to apart from His Presence). His heart transformation started with honest confession and humble acknowledgment of the Holy Spirit. You need both. It is not enough to admit to the depth of your depravity. You must also be willing to embrace His merciful grace. Present your realest self to Jesus today. Allow the Holy Spirit to guide you in your introspection. And enjoy His merciful grace.

WEEK  38

OUR COVERING

Some of my earliest school memories from Southern California are earthquake drills. Although I'm not sure what the drills look like today, when I was in elementary school, we were taught to take cover under our desks. We needed to find the most immediate physical shelter to protect our heads from any falling debris. So, during the few times a year the drill was held, we learned that the moment we felt the earth shake, we needed to look for cover. It's the perfect picture of what we tend to do when the circumstances in our lives begin to shake. When the medical test results come back uncertain or a relationship seems irreparably strained, we long to be covered and protected.

The Presence of God is the covering we seek. Because we cannot see Him in the flesh, it is easy to underestimate God as our shield. Consequently, we can find ourselves depending on people, money, and plans to protect us instead. However, time and time again in Scripture, God reminded the Israelites that He was their protector, and to remain under His protection, they had to seek and abide in His will. Isaiah 30:2 says, "Without asking my advice they set out to go down to Egypt in order to seek shelter under Pharaoh's protection and take refuge in Egypt's shadow." Here, God confronted His people for turning to other sources for refuge. It was personal to Him when He witnessed His own children display greater confidence in Egypt than in His Presence. Can God use other people and things to guard us? Absolutely. However, it is not the provision of God that covers us; it is God Himself. How do we seek Him as our refuge and shield? We approach the Presence of God with our fears, inquire of Him for help and wisdom, and follow His lead.

ACKNOWLEDGE
JESUS

_____
_____
_____
_____
_____
_____
_____
_____
_____
_____

POUR OUT
YOUR HEART

_____
_____
_____
_____
_____
_____
_____
_____
_____
_____

MEDITATE

PSALM 91:1-7

REFLECT

God Himself is the protector. The safest place to be is in the shadow of His wings—His Presence. Note how all the action verbs in this psalm are committed by God! He is not passive. He is the One who rescues, covers, and shields. He is not a bystander to our lives; He is personally invested in our well-being. Those who dwell with Him and run to Him will find a fortress of protection. To see this only as a physical guarantee would be to limit the scope of God's actual protection, for He is able to shield us on all levels, including spiritually. How God protects is beyond our understanding at times. Friend of God, you may have experienced moments when you have felt gravely let down by Jesus. The common question during these times is: "If God were really with me, why did He allow such and such to happen?" This question can callous our hearts with distrust in God. You may not fully understand *how* God is protecting you. However, you can be sure that His eyes are on every detail and angle, and He is, indeed, protecting those who abide in His Presence. Can you lean on Him and turn to Him as your most trusted covering? What does this wholehearted dependence look like specifically for you and your life?

PRAY

WEEK ✤ 39

TRUST GOD WITH THE RESULTS

When the future is unclear, angst becomes an unwelcome guest. When you are not sure if a plan will work out or how to make ends meet, an uncomfortable tension rises within. What can we do? What can we say? Our survival instinct kicks in, leading us to hustle and strive to compensate for what we cannot control. After all, anxiety is a sadistic comfort blanket because worry makes us feel like we are addressing the problem as we brood about it. The most frequent command in the Bible is "Fear not," but how do we obey this when so much is at stake?

Ultimately, we want to control the outcome of our worries. Do you ever find yourself zoning out because you are running through possible outcomes in your mind or keeping an eye on certain people so that you can micromanage the situation? We want the estranged loved one to return to us. We want the risks to be worth it. We want that one person to understand. We want the results to be in our favor. We are concerned about the outcome, and yet that is exactly what we cannot control. Friend of God, there is one thing you can do amid anxiety: *Trust God with the results.* Yes, I know that is a tough pill to swallow, but here it is again. It is not up to us to dictate how things should turn out. That is in God's hands—His gentle, merciful, and all-knowing hands. What we can determine to do today is be faithful stewards of the responsibilities and decisions that are right before us. What is up to us is our faithfulness to God and His Word. After that, we leave it at His feet. The burden to produce the best outcome is not on you. It is on your Good Friend.

ACKNOWLEDGE
JESUS

_____
_____
_____
_____
_____
_____
_____
_____
_____
_____

POUR OUT
YOUR HEART

_____
_____
_____
_____
_____
_____
_____
_____
_____
_____

MEDITATE
DANIEL 3:13-18

REFLECT

The setting for today's passage is the Babylonian occupation of Jerusalem. King Nebuchadnezzar ordered some of the Israelites of royalty and nobility to relocate to his own land to serve in his palace. They were stripped of their traditions and their way of life. The chief eunuch even renamed them to assimilate them into the Babylonian culture and religion. The glorious years of the kingdom of Israel were gone. Now, they were servants to a foreign king with very little agency over their own lives. Nevertheless, there was one thing that could not be quenched with coercion: the faith of some who chose to remain loyal to God no matter the risk. You are free to choose faith in any circumstance. The king threatened Shadrach, Meshach, and Abednego with the excruciating fate of a burning furnace if they did not submit to his god. Anyone who is up against the wall like this can feel that they have no choice but to compromise their faith. But these three refused. They did not even entertain the threat with negotiations of their own. Instead, they chose to do what honored God *with no guarantee of what was to come.* The fortitude of their faith was not dependent on whether God was willing to save them, for the goal of faith is not to just get what we want from Him. Friend of God, you have permission from heaven to do your best, remain faithful to Him, and let go of the outcome.

PRAY

WEEK  40

REMAIN WITH GOD

When bad things happen one after the other, going to God can almost feel pointless. You hope to see healing and end up dealing with a death. You pray for progress, but the situation looks like it is getting worse. What is the point of going to God when the circumstances don't show that He cares about what we need? Early in my faith, it was hard for me to reconcile how a good God could allow terrible things to happen. I was experiencing a disillusionment in my faith journey and did not know how to pray. When I asked, "What do You want from me, Father?" it was because I felt abandoned and dismissed by Him. If this was a test for great faith, I was failing. If this was spiritual warfare, I was losing. I was experiencing the mysteries of a friendship with Jesus. This is the tension between what we thought we knew and what we currently feel, when what we learned of Him in the Bible doesn't match what we're experiencing in real life.

The mystery is not where God hides but rather where He invites us to draw closer. Because He is boundlessly glorious, we cannot perfectly encapsulate Him in our finite understanding. When you find yourself entangled in mystery, God is positioning you to receive a deeper revelation of His love. To fully experience this, you must not distance yourself from Him when you are frustrated by what you cannot understand. Instead, *remain.* I know this part isn't always easy, friend. It can look like continuing to pray and linger in His Presence, even if the prayers come out as protests and questions. It can look like obedience amid doubt. It can look like returning to His Presence even after a season of hiding from Him. He is working, and His ways are higher than our ways (Isaiah 55:8–9). Immediate answers are not guaranteed, but His nearness always is.

ACKNOWLEDGE
JESUS

_____
_____
_____
_____
_____
_____
_____
_____
_____
_____

POUR OUT
YOUR HEART

_____
_____
_____
_____
_____
_____
_____
_____
_____
_____

MEDITATE
HOSEA 2:14-20

REFLECT

Hosea was a prophet when Israel was in grave rebellion and disobedience. God allowed Hosea to marry an unfaithful woman named Gomer to demonstrate to Israel how He felt toward them. Although Hosea was wholly committed to her from the start, she did not remain with him. She left him to prostitute herself to other lovers, and eventually Hosea had to buy her back. Was Hosea's love not enough? Was she disappointed by him? Did she have other desires outside the marriage? Although it is easy to judge her, one can ask the same questions to modern-day Christians as well. Eventually Hosea forgave and restored Gomer, just as the Lord intended to forgive Israel. All she had to do was go back to being Hosea's, and she was able to experience a deeper revelation of his commitment to her. Today's passage is rich with romance. Even though God's people failed to be faithful, the Lord's intention to love them endured. To experience this love, they just had to return to Him and remain. He will do the restoring. He will do the healing. He will commit Himself to His beloved, even when her commitment is frail and fickle. So, what does God want of us? He just wants us to be His. Remain. Stay in conversation with Him. Keep loving others for Him. Keep opening up that Bible. Don't run like Gomer. And if you did or do run, return. *God is not done* revealing His love for you. He will never be done, for we will be enjoying His devotion for eternity.

PRAY

WEEK  41

POUR OUT YOUR GRIEF

Enjoying the Presence of God during pain can feel impossible. Many times, pain is merciless. Whether you experience the harsh sting of rejection or the heavy sorrow of regret, pain does not care about your limitations. You may not have much appetite for praising God and doing all the "right" things with the little energy you have left after grappling with hurt.

I once watched, in horror, as someone got caught up in a rip current at the beach. His strokes and kicks did not stand a chance against the ocean's push toward the deep. Even when the lifeguards arrived, he kept flailing his arms and fighting the waves. He was pulling down the rescuers and exacerbating the emergency. Fighting the waves was draining him of survival energy and preventing him from receiving the help he needed. He had to let go. Although it makes perfect sense to us who have two feet on solid ground, it felt like a risk for him. He had to lean back and trust the strength of those around him. He had to stop fighting the waves.

Similarly, some of us expend so much energy fighting pain that we end up drowning in it. The Holy Spirit is our Comforter and Helper, but we may not experience Him in this manner when we are trying to comfort and help ourselves. Perhaps it is time to lean into Him and allow pain to run its course through you. You see, we can acknowledge our pain while also acknowledging the Presence of God. How? We grieve *with* Him. We mourn our losses openly and honestly before Jesus. We allow the mess to overflow into His courts. We pour out the pain until all that is left within us is praise.

ACKNOWLEDGE
JESUS

_____
_____
_____
_____
_____
_____
_____
_____
_____
_____

POUR OUT
YOUR HEART

_____
_____
_____
_____
_____
_____
_____
_____
_____
_____

MEDITATE

JONAH 2

REFLECT

Jonah was in the belly of the fish for three days and three nights. Because the prayer in today's passage preceded his release, one can only imagine the toil he endured before coming to this great surrender. Here he was, literally trapped in the consequence of his defiance. Although the sailors tossed him overboard into the sea, Jonah recognized it was God's love that was chastening him in this hour. Utter desperation sparked Jonah's cry to God. But as Jonah remembered Him, he did not ignore his own plight. Instead of grieving on his own, he chose to grieve with God. No matter where you cry out from, whether it is from the belly of a fish or on the floor of your bathroom, God will answer. He will not leave you alone when you pour out your heart. Eventually, Jonah gave a sacrifice of praise. It was a sacrifice because it wasn't easy to give. A sacrifice of praise comes when you are willing to abandon your comfort and pride to worship God. Jonah did not get there right away. He grieved with God first. He grieved until he was able to lift his eyes to heaven with a voice of thanksgiving. Friend of God, are you fighting any sort of pain today? Are you tired of the fight? Instead of fighting it, let's pour it out. Start with addressing how you feel. If it helps, begin with your most surface-level thoughts and emotions, and go deeper from there. Write them down or say them out loud. Perhaps, in between your confessions or afterward, allow space for the Holy Spirit to encourage you as well.

WEEK  42

FIX YOUR EYES

A few years ago, I went to Orlando with my family to visit the various amusement parks there. I was surprised to see just how much had changed over the years. So many of the rides now use virtual reality technology, where you are placed in a seat that moves and takes in artificially produced sensory experiences like wind and splashes of water. You are given goggles and seated before a screen to visually escape into another world. I thought it would feel like watching a short movie clip, but I was surprised to find how immersive the experience actually was. It really did feel like I was on a roller coaster with Minions or flying in Pandora! Yet when the lights turn back on and you get to look around, you realize you never really went anywhere. You were always in a room on a small chair. All that we felt during these rides was determined by what we were staring at (with the help of a few artificial tricks to play with our senses, of course).

Where your eyes go determines what you experience, for your soul's gaze will direct your emotions. What you fixate on will shape how you feel. This is why when we are sitting around at home, we can still be fraught with worry because our minds are fixed on what could go wrong. Even when you are busy with work, your heart can marinate on what happened in your past. The moment you wake up, you can be absent of any motivation because you've become numb through regularly scrolling social media on your phone. Where the eyes of your heart choose to linger will also condition your faith because our faith is only fortified when our eyes are fixed on Jesus. Friend of God, where are your eyes today?

ACKNOWLEDGE
JESUS

_____
_____
_____
_____
_____
_____
_____
_____
_____
_____

POUR OUT
YOUR HEART

_____
_____
_____
_____
_____
_____
_____
_____
_____

MEDITATE

MATTHEW 14:22-32

REFLECT

The disciples were in the storm because they obeyed Jesus's direction to immediately get in the boat. Not all hardship is a result of our disobedience or failure. Obeying Jesus will always be worth it, but it does not guarantee an easy life. The mysterious miracle is that Jesus walked on the very waves that were battering the disciples' boat. He was walking atop the very chaos that was scaring them. The disciples were so immersed in fear that they could not recognize Jesus as He came toward them on the water. They assumed He was a ghost. When our eyes have been staring at a storm for enough time, we may not be able to enjoy the friendship we have with Jesus. We may not even recognize His closeness! When Peter saw Jesus and received the invitation to come to Him, he was able to have dominion over the waves as Jesus did. But his eyes had to be fixed on Jesus; when he "saw the strength of the wind," fear overpowered his faith (verse 30). When his attention was on Jesus, he was able to do as Jesus did and walk on top of the very thing that scared him. Life will always compete with our heavenly gaze. Faith grows as we fix our eyes on Jesus. Has there been a storm or a problem at the center of your attention lately? How can you bring Jesus to your attention more often this week?

PRAY

WEEK ❋ 43

Enjoying friendship with God sets you free from the opinions of others. You know your awareness of His Presence is getting richer when you are more attuned to His thoughts of you than other people's assumptions. None of us can be authentically ourselves and accrue a 100 percent approval rating from those around us. Even Jesus didn't achieve that while on earth. Nonetheless, the jeers and jabs did not halt His ministry because everything He did on earth was an overflow of His secure identity as God's Son. Before His ministry even began, Jesus got baptized before His Father and a voice from heaven said, "This is my beloved Son, with whom I am well-pleased" (Matthew 3:17). The sting of disapproval cannot penetrate our hearts if we are too filled with and busy relishing God's love for us.

We can get so caught up in earning approval, trying not to disappoint others, and elevating our name. Let's be honest. What other people say about us has an effect, even if we've tried hard to develop thick skin. It hurts even more if it's from those we respect and love. Friend of God, no matter the distress of exclusion or disconnection, you can turn up your attentiveness to His nearness. Lean in for His thoughts. Perhaps you have become numb in order to block out what hurts you because it is one way to turn down the volume of other people's opinions. When we harden our hearts to the negativity, we can also keep ourselves from enjoying God's loving-kindness. Sometimes the bravest thing to do is to refuse to callous our hearts and keep them tender before His Presence. First John 3:1 reminds us, "See what great love the Father has given us that we should be called God's children—and we are!"

ACKNOWLEDGE
JESUS

POUR OUT
YOUR HEART

MEDITATE

ACTS 5:40-42

REFLECT

In Acts 5:29, Peter and the apostles declared, "We must obey God rather than people." In response, they were flogged, threatened, and shamed for preaching the gospel. This was not just embarrassing notoriety. This was physical assault and condemnation. And yet, they rejoiced! Perhaps they recalled how Jesus taught them to anticipate persecution and be glad of it (Matthew 5:10–12). Joy emerges from pain when the purpose of our lives is our friendship with Jesus. This kind of joy cannot be cracked by unfair treatment and harassment. Although they were before the presence of the Sanhedrin, the apostles were more aware of the Presence of God! While their names were defamed, they were more interested in God being glorified. As their wounds pulsated, they had their reward in heaven in mind. The apostles lived to please their Good Friend Jesus, which is why they had a joy that only grew amid suffering. Because the apostles' sole purpose was to befriend Jesus and bring others into this friendship, they were overflowing in satisfaction from the approval they had from God, even while receiving hatred. Friend of God, are you aware of what Jesus thinks of you?

PRAY

WEEK  44

HOPE IN PAIN

Full disclosure: Like many of you, I'm not a fan of any sort of discomfort. I don't even like the "good" pain from physical exercise. I don't enjoy conflict resolution with people. I don't like getting let down. And so on. Because of this, my prayers used to be my defensive mechanism of choice. They sounded like this:

- "Jesus, please let this be a good day."
- "God, please don't let anything bad happen."
- "Lord, please let this be easy."

Listen, there is nothing inherently wrong with these prayers. We can indeed pray for God's grace and favor upon every detail of our lives. However, if these are the only prayers that matter to us, then is it possible that we are not interested in living by faith but would rather use our religion to coddle our fear of pain? Faith only grows in situations where it is needed. If our devotion to God is our way of willing a life without any sort of suffering, we are missing the point entirely. We will peak as survivors when we have been equipped by the Holy Spirit to be conquerors.

Friend of God, Christ the Redeemer can take what we face and turn it into an opportunity for great blessing. Bouncing back from a hit creates resilience. Failure can produce wisdom. Now, hardship is not something we need to pray for because living on this side of heaven will always guarantee trouble. Yet it is also not something we need to avoid because the Lord uses it for His glory and for our good.

ACKNOWLEDGE
JESUS

_____
_____
_____
_____
_____
_____
_____
_____
_____

POUR OUT
YOUR HEART

_____
_____
_____
_____
_____
_____
_____
_____
_____
_____

MEDITATE

ROMANS 5:1-5

REFLECT

You have peace with God. This alone is a great miracle afforded to us by Jesus. No matter where you have failed, He has no conflict with you, not even an underlying friction. Have you ever felt the profound comfort of being unconditionally loved by someone? Jesus secured this sort of friendship for you. Access to His grace is a great privilege for every believer. Now there is no affliction that can work *against* you. Instead, God uses the affliction to work for your good according to His purpose (Romans 8:28). This allows for biblical hope, which is a joyful expectation that a good God will do good, even in bad times. Trials may crush our personal agendas, but when we sit in the tension with God, the Holy Spirit provides a supernatural endurance that only He can give. This creates in us a heavenly perspective, a Christlike mentality that turns our desires heavenward to want the things of God more than the things of this world. Friendship with Jesus allows us to chuckle at the days to come. Because here's the truth: As long as we are on this earth, brokenness will exist. However, it will never have the final word in your story. How does this truth affect you today?

WEEK ❋ 45

BEAUTY IN WEAKNESS

There have been many nights when I confessed to God that I felt He was overestimating how strong I was and how much opposition I could take. Wouldn't it be great if God would just make you stronger, better, and wiser overnight? I used to wonder why He wouldn't. The reality is that we will face things that we cannot endure and fight battles that are beyond us. There is an old church saying that goes, "God wouldn't let you go through it unless you could handle it." Have you heard it? Unfortunately, it's based off an incorrect application of 1 Corinthians 10:13, which says, "He will not allow you to be tempted beyond what you are able." The misconception is that God only allows struggles to come our way that are within our bandwidth to handle. If this were the case, then we should only have to dig within to overcome our challenges. Anyone who has undergone a significant amount of pain knows that we absolutely undergo situations that we do not have the capacity for, which is why it is good news that the second part of the verse says, "But with the temptation he will also provide the way out so that you may be able to bear it." We do go through things we cannot handle on our own, but God provides the strength that we do not have—whether in temptations or trials.

He is not offended by our weaknesses like we are. He does not disdain our inability to be better. He is not limited by our lack. He cares more for our recognition of His grace than our ability to pull ourselves up by our bootstraps and be great. Weakness draws Him closer because it honors Him when we depend on Him. Grace makes our weaknesses a beautiful place to meet with the Holy Spirit.

ACKNOWLEDGE
JESUS

_____
_____
_____
_____
_____
_____
_____
_____
_____
_____

POUR OUT
YOUR HEART

_____
_____
_____
_____
_____
_____
_____
_____
_____
_____

MEDITATE
2 CORINTHIANS 12:6-10

REFLECT

The apostle Paul had glorious experiences with God, and we can assume that he was referring to himself as the one who "was caught up into paradise and heard inexpressible words" (2 Corinthians 12:4). Here was someone who experienced uncommon and heavenly things and could have easily impressed many. Yet this was not what he chose to boast about because it was not where his strength came from. The Scriptures never clarify what Paul's "thorn in the flesh" was. Yet we do know that the Lord did not change the circumstances for him. God answers all prayers, but not all those answers are a "yes." Instead of removing the pain, God offered more grace and power to be victorious in it instead. Instead of building Paul up to be greater, He made the friendship between them deeper. Therefore, a weak Paul was strong in the Presence of God. In turn, his weaknesses were no longer a source of remorse. Instead, his weaknesses became a reason to rejoice. Friend of God, I do not know why some of your adversities cannot just be prayed away. Yet I do know that those adversities can be a tender meeting place between you and our dear Friend Jesus. He is not ashamed of your inability to be better and stronger. Instead, He delights when you draw closer.

WEEK  46

MIRACLES IN THE MUNDANE

Oftentimes it is not the tragedies in our lives that challenge our faith but rather the mundanity. It's the everydayness of our faith journey that can make us feel like we are getting nowhere with God. You could have heard a fiery sermon about how God parted the Red Sea on YouTube, and yet He doesn't even part the traffic when you're running late on your way to the doctor's office! When there is no adrenaline-charged occasion with Him, it can feel as if you've been left empty of His Presence.

Friend of God, here's the interesting thing about the seemingly uninteresting life: There is so much more in the mundane than you may see. Not only does God work in ways that we cannot perceive, but He also determines how far the ripple effect of your obedience goes. Although Mary is one of the most iconic people in biblical history, let's not forget that most of her days were spent simply being a good mother. She likely died with a tarnished reputation, with many who knew her still doubting her story of a virgin conception. Each day had chores, errands, and responsibilities to tend to. It was typical. Common. The only spectacular thing about Mary was her obedience to God. Hundreds of years later, we still know that she lived a beautifully divine life because she said yes to the Holy Spirit. She said yes to the tough things that God had called her to. She said yes to the mystery of being in friendship with God. That yes will be remembered for all eternity and made an ordinary life forever significant.

ACKNOWLEDGE
JESUS

POUR OUT
YOUR HEART

MEDITATE

EPHESIANS 3:14-21

REFLECT

It is a wonder how Paul's letters from prison, including this one, often begin with a prayer for spiritual strength for the believers (for example, Philippians 1:9–11; Colossians 1:9–12). Although we are welcome to pray for a change of circumstance, the apostle Paul's priority was for the spiritual things, often the unseen blessings, that can only come from a friendship with God. This was the miracle that Paul was eager for—that the Ephesians grow in enjoyment of what they had in Christ. Although Paul was talking to believers, he was praying that they would experience even more of God's Presence. He prayed they would have more power and a deeper comprehension of His love, which is supernatural strength and wisdom for every Christian. Isn't that thrilling? No believer can ever claim that they have reached the apex of their enjoyment of Him because He is infinite. If you ever feel like you have plateaued in your spiritual walk, this is the perfect request to pray over yourself. Although the Ephesians already knew of saving grace, Paul contended for more than that initial knowledge. If you feel as though your Christian walk has become the same old thing each day, then it is high time for a fresh revelation of the length, width, height, and depth of His love. He is not done with us, and the way to access more of Him is through earnest prayer.

PRAY

WEEK  47

PRAY THROUGH STRESS

Stress is a bully. It arrives unwelcomed to rob us of joy. You can wake up with a light heart and bright expectations, but it takes very little for our minds to start buzzing with bothersome thoughts. Yet stressful situations tend not to be as daunting when you have something or someone dependable to turn to. For example, major financial costs can be overwhelming, but a hefty savings account may provide some solace. Deep waters aren't as scary when you have a life vest on.

Once, I was exploring a new mall, and my phone randomly shut off. I was utterly discombobulated because it was fully charged, but for some reason, it was no longer functioning. I stood there in the middle of foot traffic while pressing the right buttons, and my stress levels began to spike. It wasn't like I could look up how to troubleshoot this situation because I couldn't access the internet. I couldn't drive home because I needed GPS to find my way back. I couldn't even call my husband to help me. My mind began racing for solutions and options. It was then I realized how much confidence I placed in that little device. It was where I turned for assurance as I was navigating a new space. It failed me.

Stressful situations are inevitable. However, you do have something dependable to turn to. It will not fail you like most things would. It is prayer. Knowing that we can pray about anything and have access to God's ever-present help allows us to enjoy God even while under pressure. Funnily enough, I did turn to prayer in that moment and ended up running into an old friend at that mall who had a working phone that got me home safely!

ACKNOWLEDGE
JESUS

_____
_____
_____
_____
_____
_____
_____
_____
_____
_____

POUR OUT
YOUR HEART

_____
_____
_____
_____
_____
_____
_____
_____
_____
_____

MEDITATE

PHILIPPIANS 1:3-11

REFLECT

Again, the apostle Paul was in prison while he authored these words. His life's work was beyond the prison cell, and he was stuck without the ability to fix problems or defend his name. He was powerless in chains. And yet, he gave thanks. He was joyful. He was assured. Prayer made this possible. He could not be with the Philippians, but he prayed for them. He wanted them to grow spiritually, so he brought this request to the Father. His plans and desires were all channeled through prayer. Paul was able to depend on prayer because he was confident in Jesus. A stressful situation could not rob him of his joy because Paul knew he could confess his fears to the Holy Spirit and request help. He knew that he could present his concerns to Jesus and receive guidance. Friend of God, do you default to prayer whenever you are stressed? It is a divine pathway to enjoying your friendship with God.

PRAY

WEEK  48

WHAT DO YOU VALUE MOST?

Friend of God, what you value most determines how you process tough times. When I was a child, my family and I were road-tripping and we got into a critical car accident in the desert of Nevada. Our car was completely totaled. Most of our items were not salvageable. Even all the gift shop purchases I had in the back seat from our vacation got destroyed. But here was the thing—none of us cared about any of our stuff at the time of the accident. We hardly even looked around to see what we could salvage. My three-month-old baby sister was also in that car, and until we heard her cry out to show signs of life, no one cared to calculate the damage done to our items. After a thorough check, she showed no broken bones and not even a scratch on her body—thanks be to God! We were shaken up, but we walked away from that accident overflowing with gratitude. Sure, the lost car was a tragic inconvenience. All the broken things were unfortunate. But what we valued most at that time were each other's lives, and those were not lost. We did not despair.

What do you value most? Is it Jesus? Because something happens to us when we hold Jesus Christ as our most prized possession. We become undefeatable. Our proximity to the Holy Spirit cannot be taken away from us. If you find yourself feeling defeated these days, it may be an opportunity for you to assess what you cherish and hold most dear. Much of what you come up with may be good but not be your purpose. If the purpose of your life is to enjoy a friendship with God and know Him—intimately, authentically, and passionately—then joy can abound even through the toughest times.

ACKNOWLEDGE

JESUS

_____
_____
_____
_____
_____
_____
_____
_____
_____
_____

POUR OUT

YOUR HEART

_____
_____
_____
_____
_____
_____
_____
_____
_____
_____

MEDITATE

PHILIPPIANS 3:7-11

REFLECT

Paul lost much once he fell in love with Jesus. He was a Pharisee of high religious standing. He had stability, respect, and power. Now he was in prison for preaching the gospel. In the first two verses of our passage alone, Paul mentions loss three times. But he also mentions what he gains. The word *gain* in verse 8 has the connotation of making a profit. Knowing Christ and experiencing friendship with Him was that valuable to Paul. As a Pharisee, all Paul knew of God was rules and traditions. Yet, when he met Jesus on the road to Damascus (Acts 9), God became his heavenly companion. No matter what loss came his way, he had what he valued most, and it could not be taken away from him. He would rather suffer with Jesus than live in comfort without Him. Have you ever known a love like this? This was why Paul was able to say later in Philippians 4:12, "I know how to make do with little, and I know how to make do with a lot. In any and all circumstances I have learned the secret of being content—whether well fed or hungry, whether in abundance or in need." If Paul's friendship with God kept him content in prison, then it can cultivate a wholeness and satisfaction within you while you endure this season of your life. Even if this has not been your experience yet, you can begin with trusting that any investment into your communion with the Holy Spirit is also an investment into your joy.

PRAY

WEEK  49

REMEMBER WHO YOU ARE

"Have you been preaching, Preacher?" This was the text my dear friend sent me during one of the most chaotic and heart-wrenching periods of my life. It was 2020 and I had undergone what felt like a year of crushing. My family and I lost much and many, and the weight of the pain was paralyzing. Starting a church in this condition felt absolutely ridiculous. I did not want to make any more plans or dream any more dreams. Grief does that to you.

Despite this, I was blessed to have someone who refused to let me off the hook as I wallowed in self-pity while discounting everything the Lord has done for me over the years. When circumstances and people fail us, we tend to ignore what God has already accomplished in us. I had allowed my obstacles to define me. I thought that because I felt abandoned by some, I was alone. I thought that because I had failed, I was a failure. It took that one-sentence text to remind me that I could not afford to ignore the God-given calling over my life. I was *not* what was happening to me. Instead, I was what God did in me.

All believers have a heavenly deposit embedded within them. You are not your circumstances, nor your past. You are not your mistakes. No, dear reader, you are a friend of God. You have a story. You have spiritual gifts. You have His approval. You have everything you need to fulfill the unique mission God has designed you for. Pain and shame cannot change who you are in Christ.

ACKNOWLEDGE
JESUS

_____
_____
_____
_____
_____
_____
_____
_____
_____

POUR OUT
YOUR HEART

_____
_____
_____
_____
_____
_____
_____
_____
_____
_____

MEDITATE

2 TIMOTHY 1:1-7

REFLECT

Paul began this letter by reminding Timothy of his heritage of faith. Not only did Timothy's grandmother and mother pass down faith, but Paul also sowed into Timothy as well. There was great spiritual investment in Timothy, all of which Timothy would have been tempted to ignore when he faced the intimidation that came with being a young minister of his time (1 Timothy 4:12). The word *rekindle* in 2 Timothy 1:6 implies that Timothy needed to begin using his gifts again. Fear caused him to shrink back and forget what he carried. Thankfully he had someone to remind him that although he felt fear, he did not have the spirit of fear. In fact, Timothy had everything that he needed to fulfill God's calling in his life. It is also poignant that the people who modeled faith to Timothy were his grandmother and his mother. This legacy of faith was carried down for generations, not by celebrity preachers or the rich, but by women who faithfully believed! Do not forget who you are, friend of God. Do not forget what's been given to you by the Holy Spirit. If you need encouragement to reignite the flame, you can seek out a fellow believer in Christ to pray for you as Paul continually prayed for Timothy. How else can you reject any stagnancy that comes from fear and actively serve and love others?

PRAY

WEEK  50

EYES ON FOREVER

No wilderness season lasts forever. No hardship goes into eternity. It can feel like it, though. The weight of today suggests that there is no better tomorrow. I was once bedridden with an autoimmune disease for a few months when I was nineteen years old. Every day felt like forever. The duress of not knowing what this disease could potentially do to me was heavy. Hours in bed left me in my head for most of the day, and I found no solace there. Suffering usually touts itself to be the final word when, in reality, it is but a gust of wind in comparison to forever.

Even Jesus knew that the excruciating pain on the cross was not forever. He knew what was beyond the cross, and it gave Him the strength to endure it. It was glory for eternity spent with you! Temptations and pressures are relentlessly consuming. They pester us into being caught up in the doom of "right now." Right now, you may be hurt. Right now, you may feel lonely. Right now, you may be tired of waiting. But that's right now. This right now will not outlast God, for only God is forever. Friend of God, let's fix our eyes on forever.

ACKNOWLEDGE
JESUS

_____
_____
_____
_____
_____
_____
_____
_____
_____
_____
_____

POUR OUT
YOUR HEART

_____
_____
_____
_____
_____
_____
_____
_____
_____
_____

MEDITATE

HEBREWS 12:1-4

REFLECT

In the chapter just before this, the author lists out a "Hall of Faith," which is comprised of heroes of faith who lived not for immediate rewards but for the things to come. Faith's objective is not realized here on earth because it looks for its bounty in heaven. Faith is not the same as creating a vision board for the year's aspirations or a financial plan to buy a house. Faith dreams bigger, for it considers eternity. You love when it's hard because you consider other people's souls in heaven. You fight for a pure heart because you know that you could never gratify the temptations that our Good Friend died for. Sin is easy when you do not believe that what is beyond will be reward enough, which is why we must run this race as Jesus ran it. We must keep our eyes on the prize. Although Jesus despised the shame of the cross, He willingly endured it by considering what was ahead. It was joy that motivated Him, the joy of being reunited with the Father and making a way for us to know Him. Can you see yourself freely communing with Christ in paradise? Laughing and singing while being completely and irrevocably free? Let's look ahead. Let's gaze beyond. Let's fix our eyes on Jesus.

WEEK  51

FAITH ANCHORS

Faith anchors us to the Presence of God. You can be imprisoned by your circumstances. You can be harangued by a squall of unforeseen tragedy. You can even be bored by routine mundanity. And all the while, you can still delight in your friendship with the Holy Spirit. Faith is what keeps you there. It ensures that we remain with Him while we weep. It causes us to keep inquiring of Him when we are at a loss for what to do. It keeps us trusting Him when our plans fall through. Faith keeps us believing in the good news even while wading through bad news.

I am one of the most gullible people I know. If you were to tell me a celebrity died or that I shrunk two inches, I may seriously consider it. The thing about gullibility is that your mood sways with everything you believe! I once took a long nap on a family trip and woke up to everyone telling me that it was the next day and that I had completely missed all the activities. It made us laugh together later, but in that moment, I was so upset! Gullibility makes us so quick to believe anything, and that belief takes our emotions for a ride. In the same way, our lack of faith can be likened to spiritual gullibility. We get caught up with the whirlwind of trouble. We get washed away by our menacing worries. Instead of believing that He is with us always, we allow disheartening news to convince us that He has left us hanging. Rather than trusting that He will provide, we allow that unexpected bill to convince us that He cannot help.

Friend of God, I am certain that what you are facing this week is as real as can be, and faith does not dismiss your present-day circumstances. It simply ensures that you do not dismiss eternal promises. It anchors you to what is real, keeping you from being swayed by the first whiff of foreboding negativity.

ACKNOWLEDGE
JESUS

POUR OUT
YOUR HEART

MEDITATE
JAMES 1:2-8

REFLECT

In his letter, James calls Christians to spiritual maturity, and this is only possible by depending on our friendship with Jesus during hardship. Instead of writing, "If you experience various trials," he says, "Whenever you experience various trials." Although there are many blessings to the Christian journey, the purpose of our faith is not to build the ideal life. *There will be trials.* Yet, when we have faith amid the trials, the pain ultimately serves as gain. What does faith look like during difficulty? Hebrews 11:6 says that the one who draws near to God with faith must believe that He exists and rewards those who seek Him. In other words, we pray trusting that He is near and that He will receive us with kindness. Dear friend, do not allow tough times to convince you to ignore God. Enjoy your divine friendship today by asking Him for wisdom while trusting that He will respond with what you need.

PRAY

WEEK  52

THE HONOR OF FAITH

Friend of God, you will not need faith in heaven. Once we step onto eternity's shores, we will not need to *try* to believe. Heaven will be visible, audible, and tangible. We will not have to look for hope. It will already be fulfilled as we finally see the One we've loved in this life. You are an eternal being residing in a mortal body amid temporary problems. What will matter at the end of this life is the blood-bought friendship you have with God.

Faith is an honor we get to participate in while we live our limited days here on earth. We *get* to do this! It is our one chance to say that we believed before we saw His glory with our very eyes. It is our one opportunity to say that we gave thanks before it was easily overflowing from within us. Today, we can say we trust Him with every fiber of our aching hearts, despite not seeing Him or hearing Him. Tonight, we can say that we wrestled our flesh to obey Him, for one day our flesh will not have to try. What makes your time right now significant in redemptive history is whether you have faith. Today, you may have an ever-so-faint confidence in the Lord, but that is your faith still flickering. Hold fast to it like treasure. Honor it, for it has endured much. No matter how dimly it burns, it burns still. And it is precious to our dear Friend Jesus.

ACKNOWLEDGE
JESUS

_____
_____
_____
_____
_____
_____
_____
_____
_____
_____

POUR OUT
YOUR HEART

_____
_____
_____
_____
_____
_____
_____
_____
_____
_____

MEDITATE

1 PETER 1:3-9

REFLECT

First Peter 1:3 says that we are born again in Christ with "a living hope." The New Living Translation refers to it as living with "great expectation." It is the sort of joyful anticipation that cannot be left disappointed. It is not like hoping to get into our dream college or hoping to marry a certain kind of person. This hope cannot fade or corrode. It is a hope that gives life to those who dare to hold it. What is this hope? It is the confidence that Jesus will return and make all things new, allowing us to enjoy the culmination of our salvation at the end of days (Revelation 21). Until then, the faith we hold to is of great value to our Good Friend. It is loving Him when you cannot hear His voice. It is believing in His words when faithfulness feels like a waste of time. It is trusting that He is not done when the outlook is bleak. That faith may not seem like much at the moment, but it will be on display at the end of time.

NOTES

INTRODUCTION

1. Holman Bible Publishers, *Holman Illustrated Bible Dictionary* (Nashville, Tenn.: Holman Reference, 2003), 957.
2. Faith Eury Cho, *Experiencing Friendship with God* (Colorado Springs, Colo.: WaterBrook, 2023), 96.

ENJOYING SALVATION

1. Allen C. Myers, *The Eerdmans Bible Dictionary* (Grand Rapids, Mich.: William B. Eerdmans, 1987), 105.

ENJOYING HIS PRESENCE

1. James A. Swanson, *Dictionary of Biblical Languages with Semantic Domains: Hebrew: Old Testament* (Bellingham, Wash.: Logos Research Systems, 1997), #8264.
2. Brother Lawrence, *The Practice of the Presence of God* (New Kensington, Penn.: Whitaker House, 1982), 80.
3. Edward J. Woods, *Deuteronomy: An Introduction and Commentary*, Tyndale Old Testament Commentaries, vol. 5 (Downers Grove, Ill.: InterVarsity Press, 2011), 133–34.

ABOUT THE AUTHOR

FAITH EURY CHO'S mission is for all to enjoy the gift of the gospel, which is the Presence of God. She is the co-founder and co-pastor of Mosaic Covenant Church of New Jersey, alongside her husband, Pastor David Cho. Faith Eury Cho is the CEO and founder of the Honor Summit, a nonprofit ministry that equips and activates Asian American women for the mission of God. She and her husband have four children.